AF268516

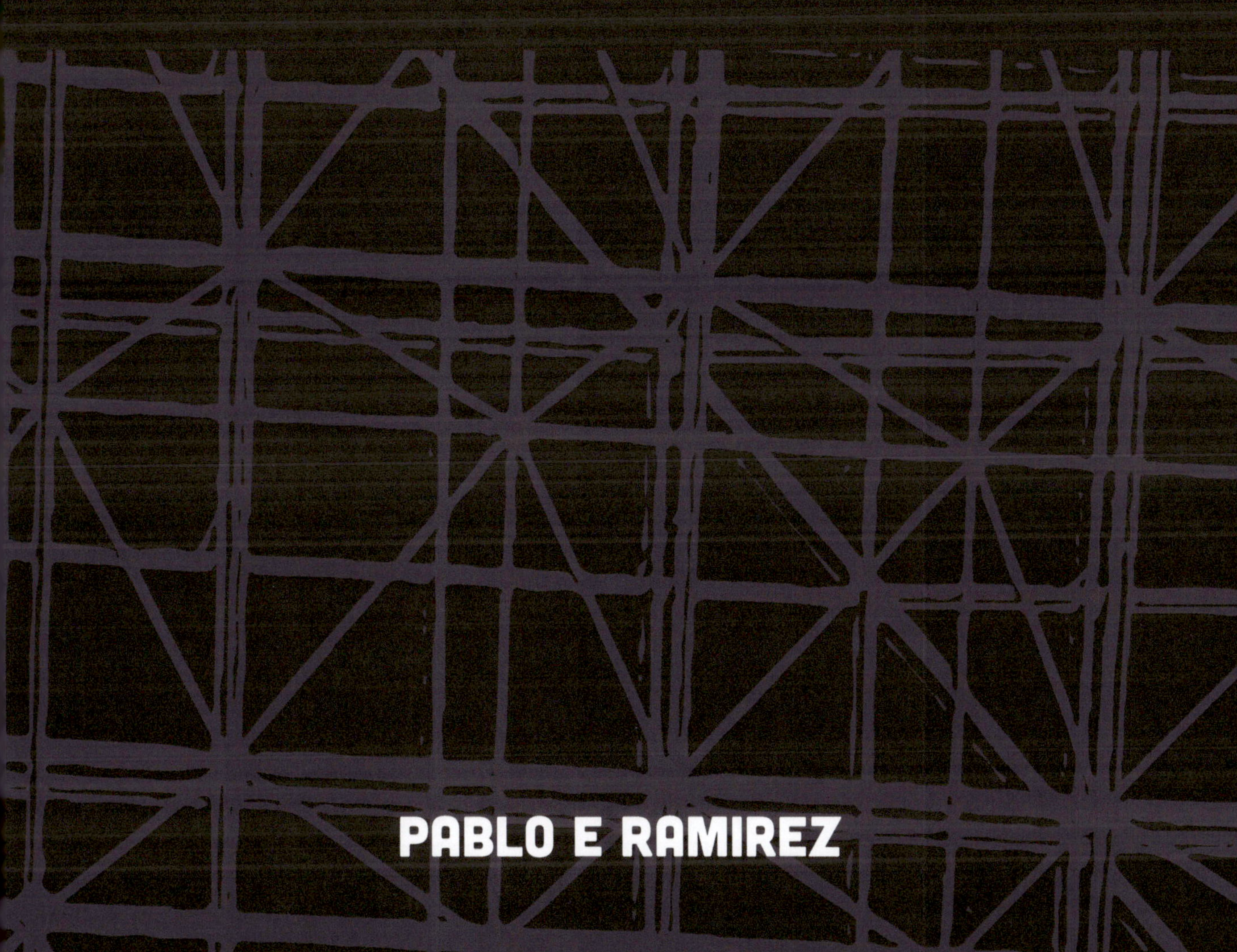

POCHO LOVE

PILSEN HEART BEATS TO CHICAGO STREETS

PABLO E RAMIREZ

POCHO LOVE
PILSEN HEART BEATS TO CHICAGO STREETS

Pocho Love/ Pilsen Heart Beats To Chicago Streets
Copyright ©2023 by Pablo Ramirez
Copyright for this edition © LACASA Books and MARCH Abrazo Press

All rights reserved. No part of this publication may be stored in a retrieval system, transmitted, or reproduced in any way, including but not limited to photocopying, photography, magnetic recording, laser or otherwise, without the prior agreement and written permission of the author.

ISBN: 978-1-877636-04-2

Preassigned Control Number (PCN) 9781877636042

Library of Congress Control Number: 2023917003

Ramirez,Pablo, 1975

Listed in the Catalogue of the Library of Congress: 1. Poetry 2. Art 3. Chicano Poetry 4. Street Art 5 Mexican-American 6 Chicago Chicano Literature 7 Latinx Literature

For readings, presentations or artist exhibitions please contact
Pablo Ramirez at 1000masks@gmail.com

www.lacasachicagobooks.org
mzimmerman1939@gmail.com

marchabrazopress@yahoo.com

Printed in United States of America

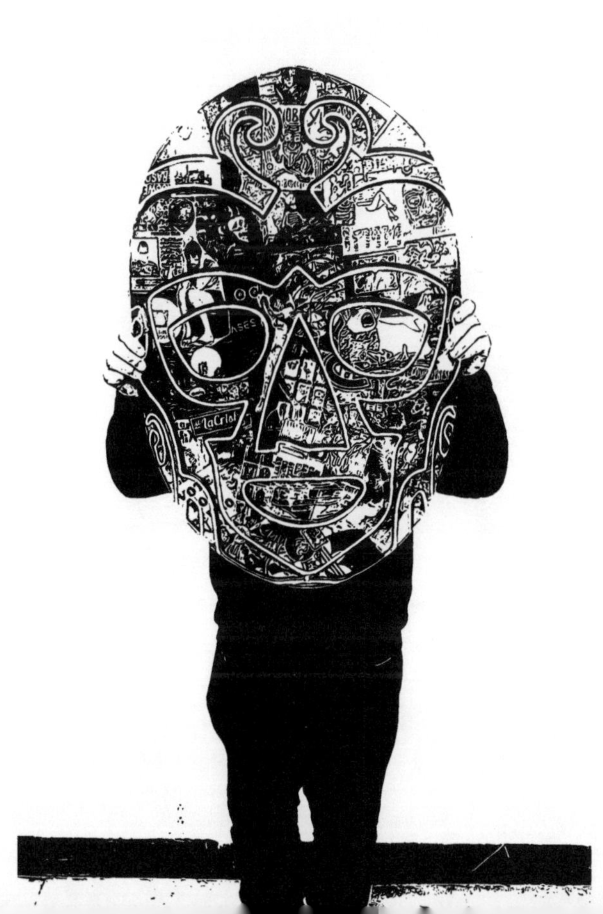

CONTENTS

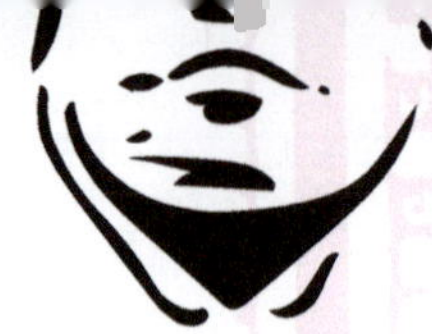

EL MONSTRO

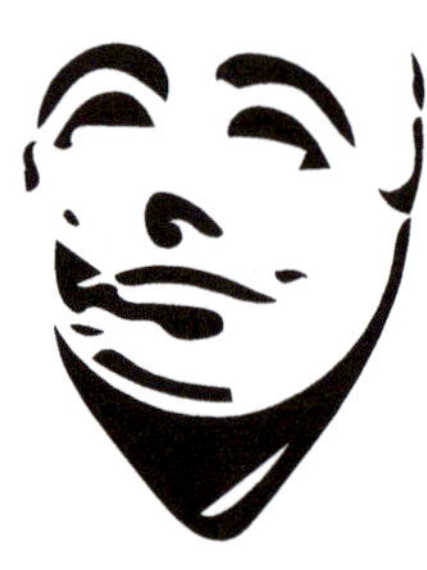

Scared of my mind
Because rhymes come alive
Hands turn dials
Arms tense up
And start to spin wheels
Sounds of classic
Chevrolet
Play like you like me
Scream that you hate me
I'm sick
Don't you understand?
Monster in the making
Poisoned by your persistence
That scent so indecent
You should bottle it
Sprayed by someone
Someday
Replayed last Monday
Televised those eyes
Screened those lies
Say something
I've never heard before

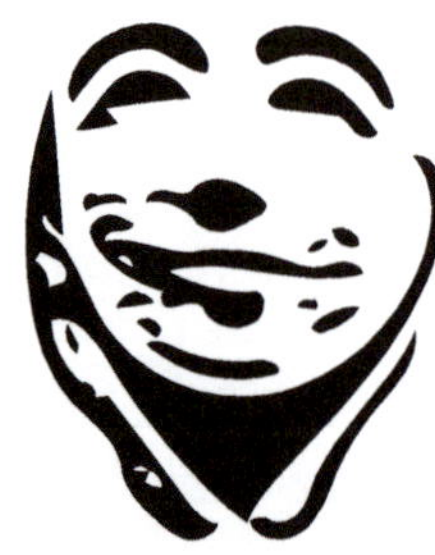

I score and taste tequila
Terrific timing
I only care
Because I miss someone
I shouldn't
Have met but meet me
Desire me damn it
Like you I'm outstanding
I fight every night
Monster in the making
I wear my mask everyday
But who notices
Otro pinche lavaplatos
Enmascarado
Triste agave
Dulce tequila
Mirror me
Because I never married
Mention me
Desire me damn it
Like you I am outstanding
I fight every night
Monster in the making.

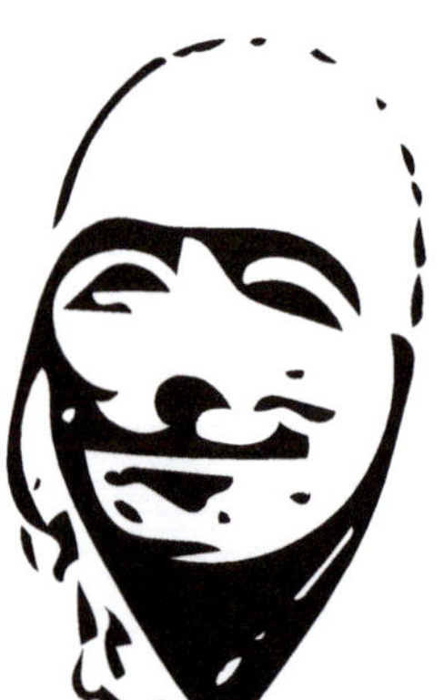

EL MONSTRO

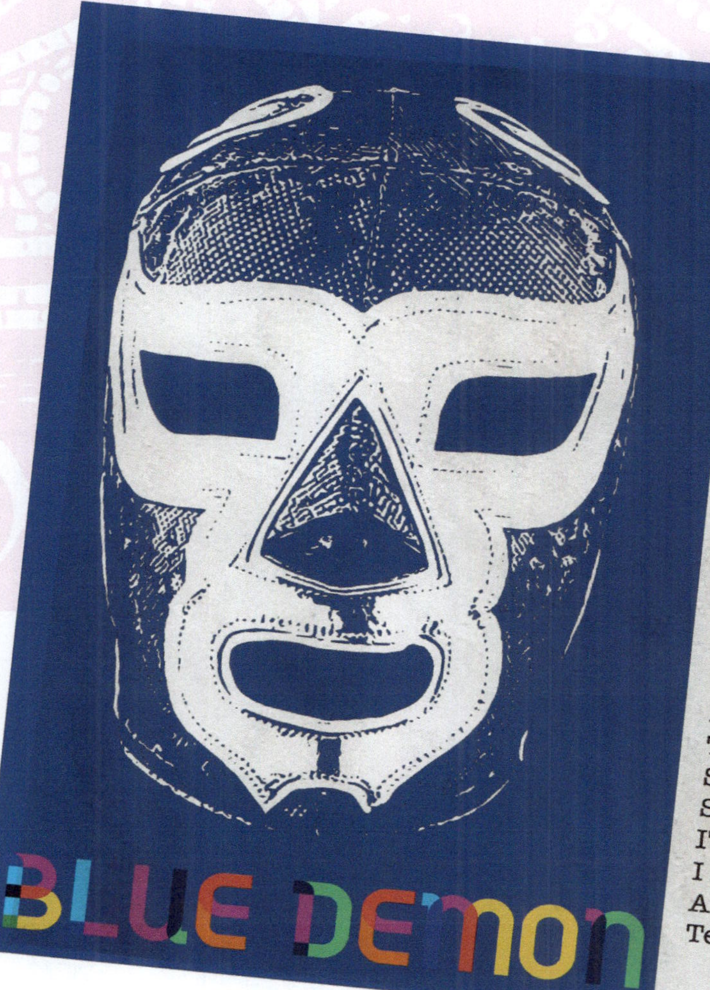

Scared of my mind
Because rhymes come alive
Hands turn dials
Arms tense up
And start to spin wheels
Sounds of classic Chevrolet
Play like you like me
Scream that you hate me
I'm sick
Don't you understand?
Monster in the making
Poisoned by your persistence
That scent so indecent
You should bottle it
Sprayed by someone /someday
Replayed last Monday
Televised those eyes
Screened those lies
Say something
I've never heard before
I score
And taste tequila
Terrific timing

I only care
Because I miss someone
I shouldn't
Have met but meet me
Desire me damn it
Like you
I'm outstanding
I fight every night
Monster in the making
I wear my mask everyday
But who notices
Otro pinche lavaplatos
Enmascarado
Triste agave
Dulce tequila
Mirror me
Because I never married
Mention me
Desire me damn it
Like you
I am outstanding
I fight every night
Monster in the making.

PILSEN PILSEN PILSEN

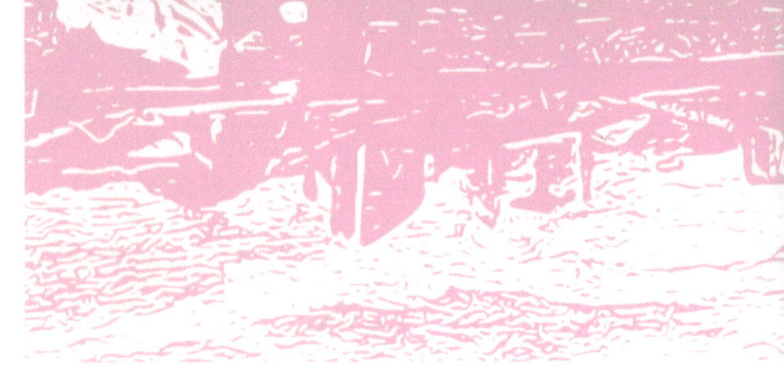

Pilsen Pilsen Pilsen Pilsen
Pilsen Pilsen Pilsen
Pilsen Pilsen Pilsen Pilsen
Pilsen Pilsen Pilsen
PILLLZZZEN
Is a city in the Czech Republic
But My Pilsen
Looks like me
Was born in the 70s
And grew up in the 80s on 17th
My Pilsen
Grew up in gangways
Played fast pitch behind a potato factory
And braved train tracks at too early an age
My Pilsen
Played catch one catch all
Kicked the can
And jumped off garages
To run away from my friends
Braved going to the hot dog spot
And played Mario Bros and flipped turtles
Was there when Pizza Nova opened
and satisfied with a 99 cent slice
That left the plate invisible
My Pilsen
Was of Romero, Raya, Vega, Ayala ,
Lozano, Gonzalez ,Mendoza & Solis
Diana no el otro güey
My Pilsen
Tenia Abuelo y Bigote
Cortez y cigarros
Sombrero y botas
Sonrisa y enseñanza
My Pilsen
Lo estraña
Y le hace falta
For those who don't know
Pilsen has boundaries but is infinite
But in case you are wondering
16th, Halsted , Cermak, Blue Island,

Western
My Pilsen is Female
But is uncomfortable using pronouns
My Pilsen
Had a baby with La Villita
And named it Marshall
Ok we had an East Pilsen too
Pero realmente no cuenta
Y ahora
Este Pilsen
Is colorblind
but hates white
And gossips when black is around
Este Pilsen
Has a fest every weekend
and doesn't know if that's good or not
Mole, Tacos, Conchas, Miches, Sabores
Tacos y Tamales, House y *Pinche* Fest
Este Pilsen is aware of its
International status
But doesn't care for bloggers
Or journalists
Or *babosos*
Que dicen tonterías por el internet
Este Pilsen
Corazón de la ciudad
Venas como hilos frágiles
Se empiezan a deshacer
Como mis recuerdos
Bellos de cultura bella que baila
Y murales que nos enseñaban
De los grandes
And now
This Pilsen
Bleeds
Shoots people *sin miedo*
Sweats like summer viaducts
And stinks like *borrachos*
This Pilsen
Would rather run you over

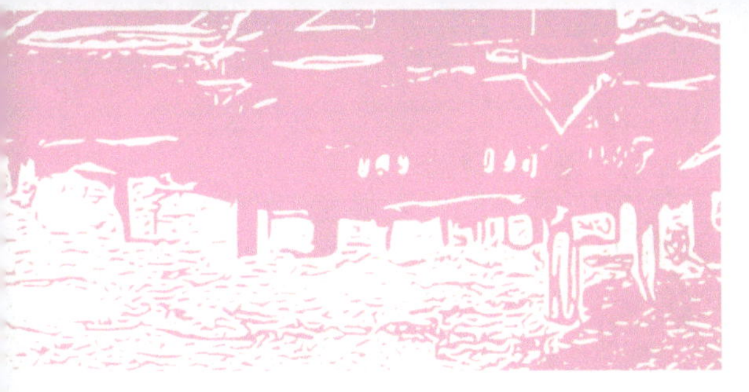

Than say hello
This Pilsen is color coded
And gray means you are not
community even if your *paisa*
This Pilsen
Se *vende pedacito por pedacito*
And beats its employees
And its partners
And pays undocumented workers
less than minimum wage
Triste y sin pena
Celebramos con Modelos
Y Coronas y platos de 10 dolares
Pilsen Pilsen Pilsen Pilsen Pilsen
Pilsen PilsenPilsen Pilsen Pilsen
Pilsen Pilsen Pilsen Pilsen
Pinche pinche pinche fest
My Pilsen
Cuanto te quiero y no te puedo dejar
Of Action, of Magaña, of Barberena of Perez
Of Ramirez , García y Serment y Solis
Diana no el otro pendejo.

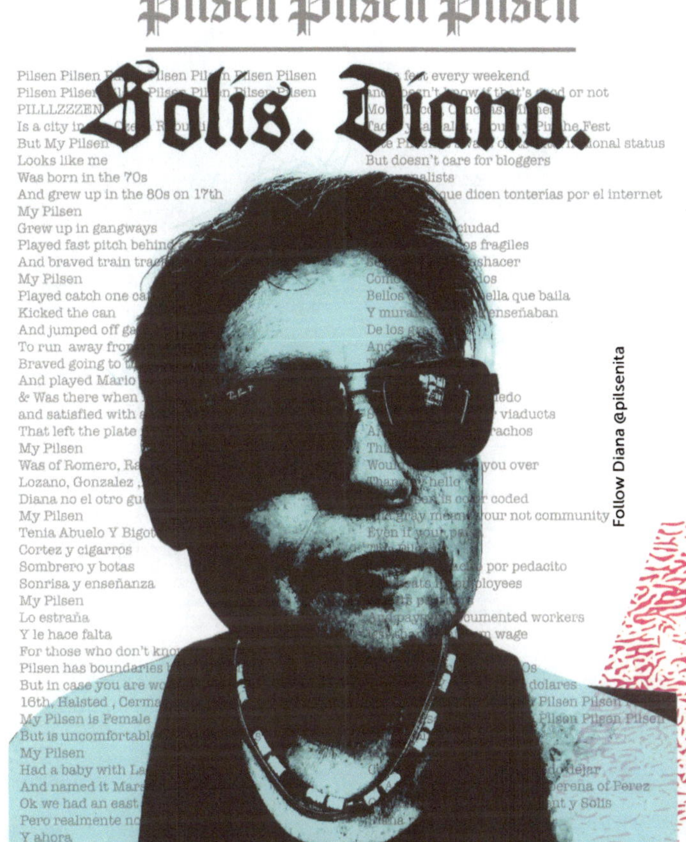

Follow Diana @pilsenita

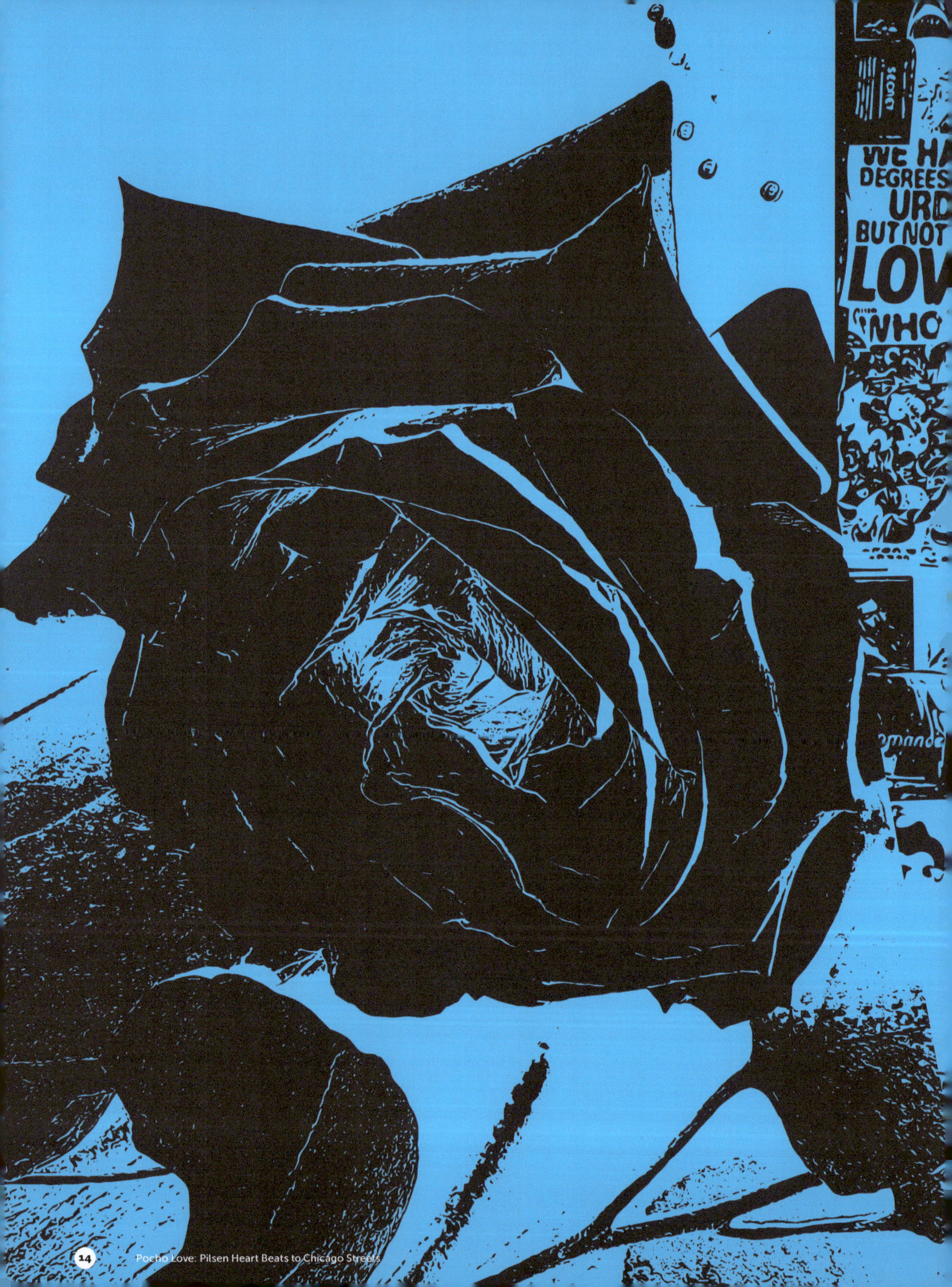

WE HA
DEGREES
URD
BUT NOT
LOV
WHO

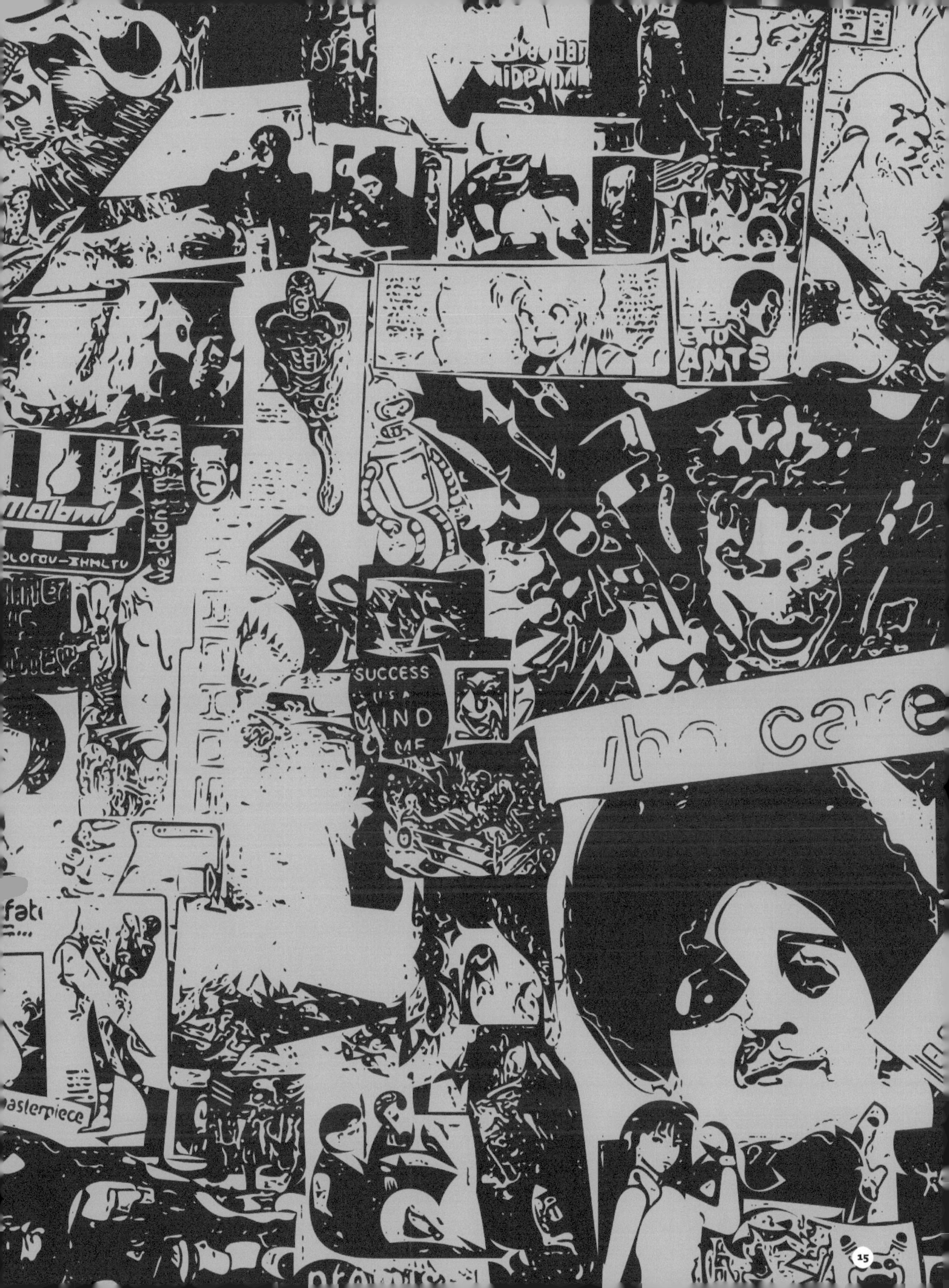
SUCCESS
IS A
MIND ME
who care
masterpiece
ANTS

RETIRED POET

When I was a poet
I was really green, I mean really green
Not that fake blue bag bullshit
some of you and Daley are on
I would wake up on a bed
of scorching sand and rock
In an Arizona desert
I showered *debajo cascadas* of *Texolo*
I ate only *tunas* from the barbed *nopal*
I played catch and fetch
with *águilas* and *serpientes*
When I was a poet
I used to ride the C.T.A.
In search of blurry colored visions of you
And then you would appear
like bible prophecy
Boricua Goddess, I put ink to paper
And the rest was history
We belonged like *horchatas to taquerías*
Like *arroz y habichuelas con chuletas*
Our love lassoed two communities
Pilsen and Humboldt Pk.
Shit, when I was a poet
I put those two places on the map.
I invented words because I had a license
And said cool shit like
"I want to hold you
like a handle does a mug"
And you would do it.
Or would meet unemployed playmates
and tell them
"holding you is like holding money".
And then let them slip away
después de unos besos.
When I was a poet
April, May and June
weren't just months in a year
They were viejas that wanted some
Y Julia wasn't very shy either.
Always paging me.

That's right!
Because when I was a poet
All poets carried pagers like doctors
Because we were always on call.
When I was a poet
I was both Armitage and Roscoe St.
When David would yell
I would yell with him
"Ammeeriicooooo"
And when he would read Chitown Brown
I felt like he was talking about me.
When I was a poet
Armadillos and coyotes, Cumpián and I
Would gather around in circle
He used to recite poems about my
moms *pozole* or talk about
How he was in the Black Panther Party.
Muy Chingón!
Then I would read some of my
pocho love poems
And he would grade them.
He always gave me C's.
¿Ese güey qué sabe?
When I was a poet
Every New Years Eve
Was spent in Cortez' living room *museo*
Artists, Activists, Poets, Low-lifes,
Revolucionarios,
Children, Socialists, Teachers, *Borrachos*
and one or two occasional federal agents
Shared piping hot chili and
when midnight hit
We would bless the four divine directions
with the sacred concha.
When I was a poet
I was a card carrying member of the
Royal Chicano Air Force
I lived *veinte años of joda* like Montoya
And that was only the beginning
I loved like Pablo

Howled with Allen
Backpacked with Jack
And fucked like Bukowski
I even lived on Mango St.
Y mi nombre era Joaquín
When I was a poet
I always had a front row seat
at Latino Chicago
Chicago Chicano Prince
I too wore a phallic mask during
Short Eyes
And burned and cried
When Damen died
And when Gregorio got his
motorcycle I would wait for him
to pass out and take his *ruka* and his
bike out for a ride on Lakeshore Drive.
When I was a poet
I was *Indio, Jaguar, Mexica*
I fought colonization, gentrification,
capitalismo y racismo
With poisoned arrows
Blue eyes were the bullseye
And I was always on target
Not a mistake or creation of hate
Only self defense from cultural rape
When I was a poet
Simile, hyperbole, personification and
alliteration
Were words wannabe poets
used to throw around
When I was a poet
I was art, ink and beauty
Era la verdad, mentiras y promesas
I was the anti-politician
I was proud to step on stage
and show my face
And I was proud to hide my face
with a mask in a Chiapas jungle
When I was a poet
I dreamt of this exact moment
I woke up born again everyday
I rocked, slammed and preached
I kissed crowds
When I was a poet.

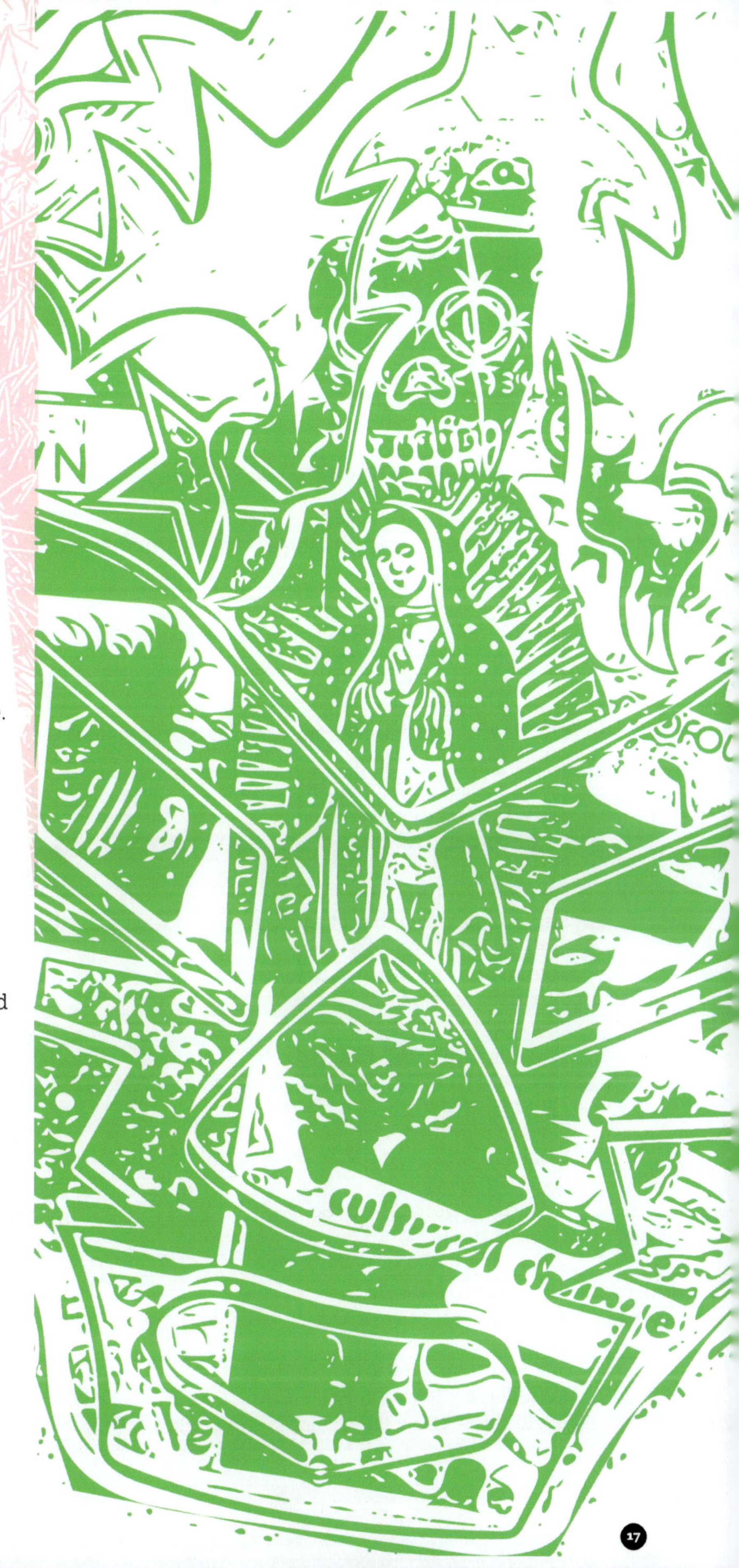

PANCITA

Why you so afraid?
What do you see that I don't know
What is that fucking heart doing
When I speak
Sleeping, beating, resting, bursting
Bleeding most likely
Wet like 2011 Chicago
Wake up . *Despierta chingado*
Do you have a Daley *cruda*
Huevos con chorizo
That's what Mexicanos do
My stomach can't stomach
floating stomach
Menudo might be
What my doctor prescribed
When we were in love
It was a Monday after a Bears victory
But we aren't in love
So why you so afraid
Is it my eyes, have they told lies?
Do they smother you?
Should I put a leash on them?
Dogs without masters
Like my city's aldermen
Dirty like *favelas*
One day I hope to visit
That bleeding spot again
So I can taste your fear
Fear me? Why?
Is it my words
What if I could not speak
Rap with lazy beats
Would my words have teeth
Or be discreet?
Because you never have been
And I wouldn't want that
Tainted temptress
To visit me again
Sin permiso, pero la cabrona
tiene llave y tiene miedo
And I don't know why.

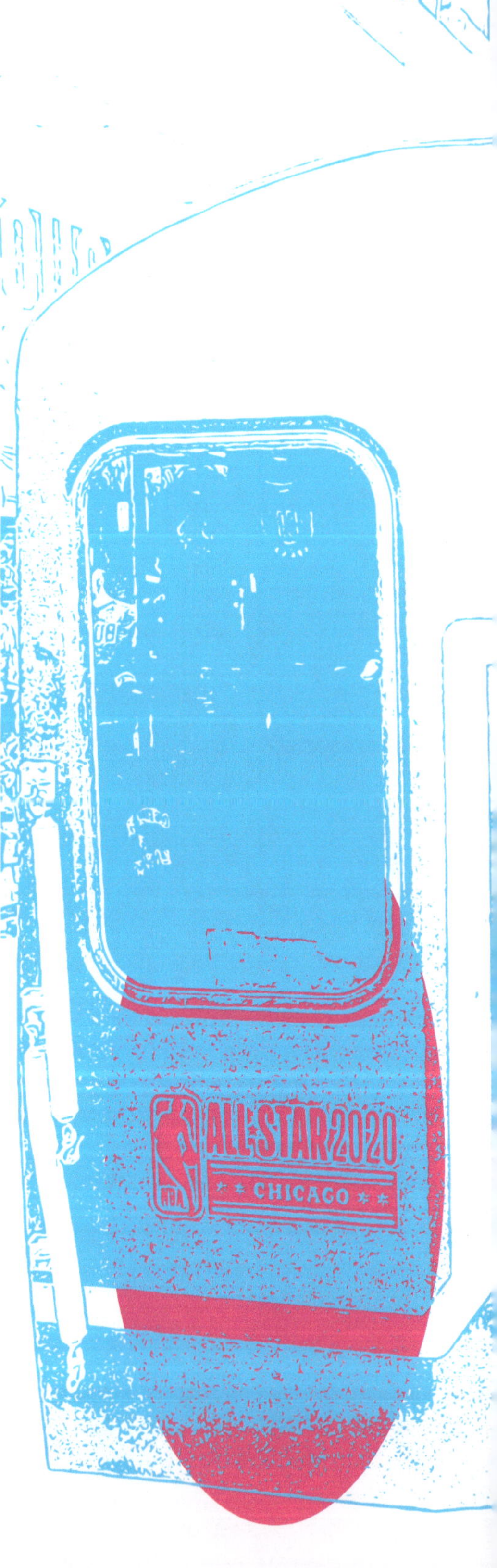

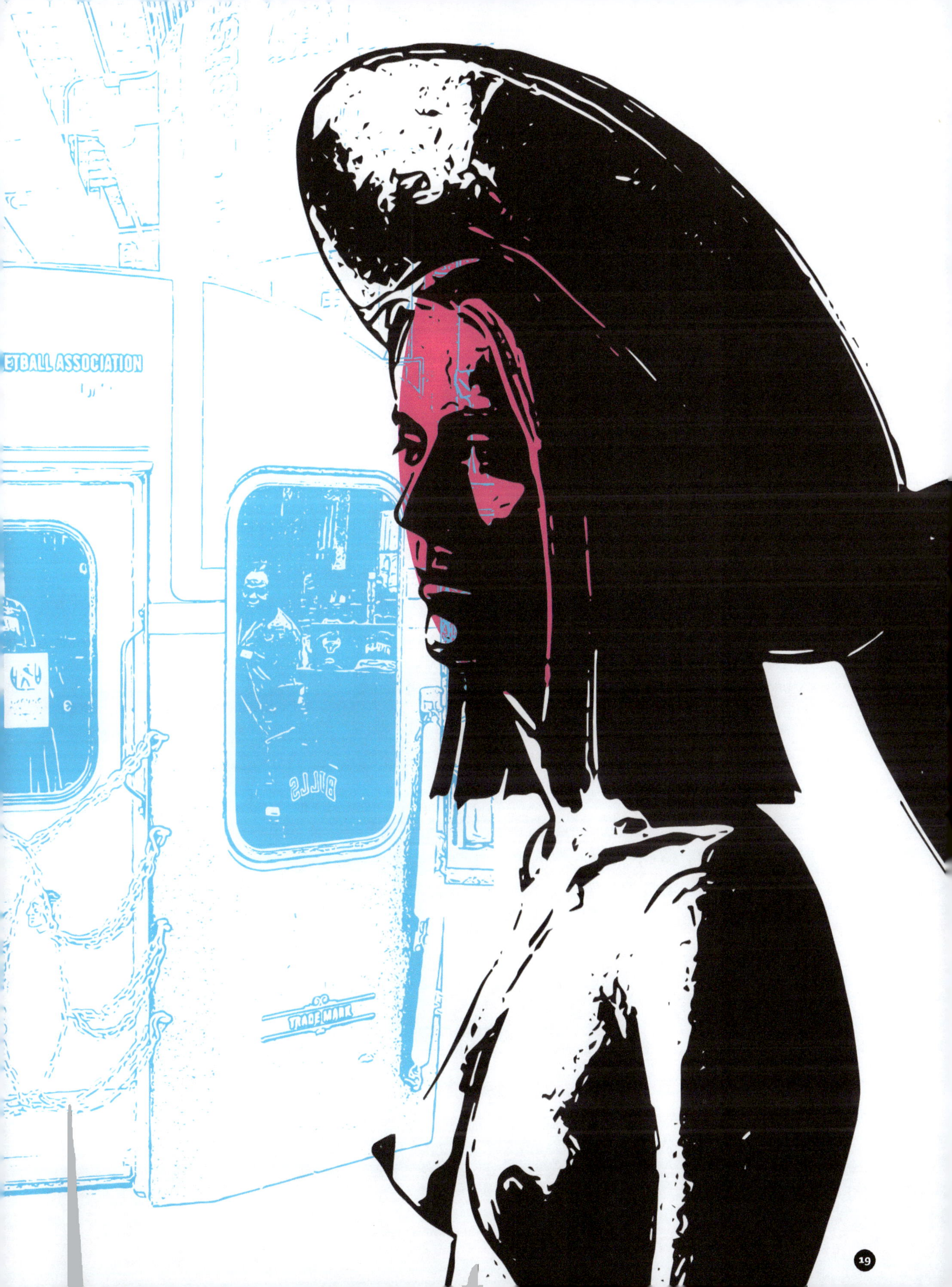
ETBALL ASSOCIATION
BILLS
TRADE MARK

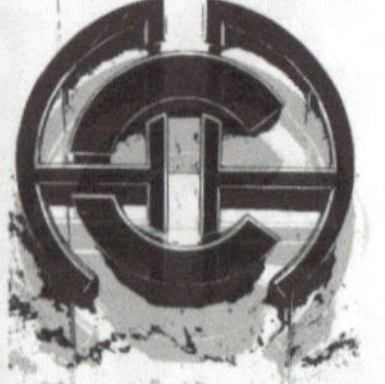

Corner Chronicles

MF DOOM DEAD. MF

Livin' off borrowed time, the clock tick faster
That'd be the hour they knock the slick blaster
Dick Dastardly and Muttley with sick laughter
A gun fight and they come to cut the mixmaster
I-C-E cold, nice to be old
Y2G steed twice to threefold
He sold scrolls, lo and behold
Know who's the illest ever like the greatest stor
Keep your glory, gold and glitter
For have half of his ni**az'll take him out the pic
The other half is rich and don't mean sh*t-ta
Villain a mixture between both with a twist of liquor
Chase it with more beer, taste it like truth or dare
When he have the mic it's like the place get like: 'Ah yea
It's like they know what's 'bout to happen
Just keep ya eye out, like aye, aye cap'n
Is he still a fly guy clappin' if nobody ain't hear it
And can they testify from innor spirit (no)

In living, the true
Givin' y'all nothing but the lick like two br
Got more lyrics than the church got 'Ooh L
An e old the mic and your attention like two sw
Or even one with two blades
Hey you, don't touch the mic like it's AIDS
It's like the end to the m
F*cked type of message that sends to the fi
That's why he brings his own nee
nd get more cheese than Doritos, Cheetos or F
Slip like Freu
r first and last step to playin' yourself like accor
When he at the mic you don't go
Even pussy cats like why hoes need K
Exercise index won't need Bow
nd won't take the one with no skinny legs like Joe

DJBooth ✔ @DJBooth · Dec 31, 2020

#MFDOOM was one of one. There will never be another like him. Rest easy, Daniel Dumile.

"His raps are stream-of-consciousness mind dumps that owe as much to Marvel's Stan Lee as they do to Kool Keith." -@CineMasai_

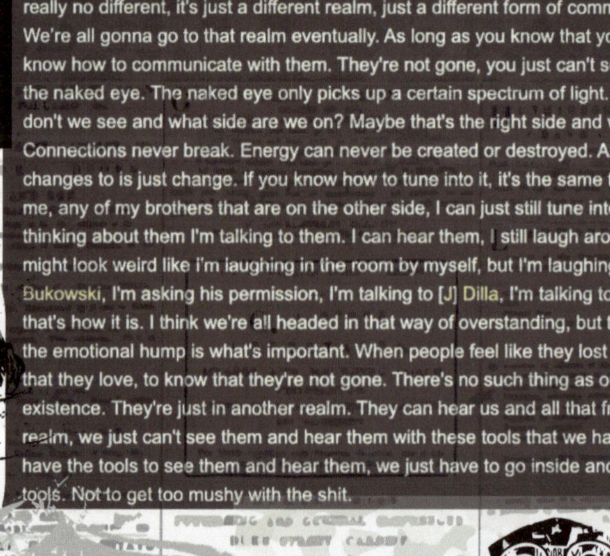

DX: Is it hard for you to channel that essence with your brother being gone?
DOOM: Anytime you lose a family member there's a grieving period. But it's no really no different, it's just a different realm, just a different form of communica We're all gonna go to that realm eventually. As long as you know that you can know how to communicate with them. They're not gone, you just can't see the the naked eye. The naked eye only picks up a certain spectrum of light. What don't we see and what side are we on? Maybe that's the right side and we're g Connections never break. Energy can never be created or destroyed. Anything changes to is just change. If you know how to tune into it, it's the same thing. me, any of my brothers that are on the other side, I can just still tune into them thinking about them I'm talking to them. I can hear them, I still laugh around th might look weird like i'm laughing in the room by myself, but I'm laughing with Bukowski, I'm asking his permission, I'm talking to [J] Dilla, I'm talking to Sub. that's how it is. I think we're all headed in that way of overstanding, but to get the emotional hump is what's important. When people feel like they lost some that they love, to know that they're not gone. There's no such thing as out of existence. They're just in another realm. They can hear us and all that from th realm, we just can't see them and hear them with these tools that we have. Or have the tools to see them and hear them, we just have to go inside and utilize tools. Not to get too mushy with the shit.

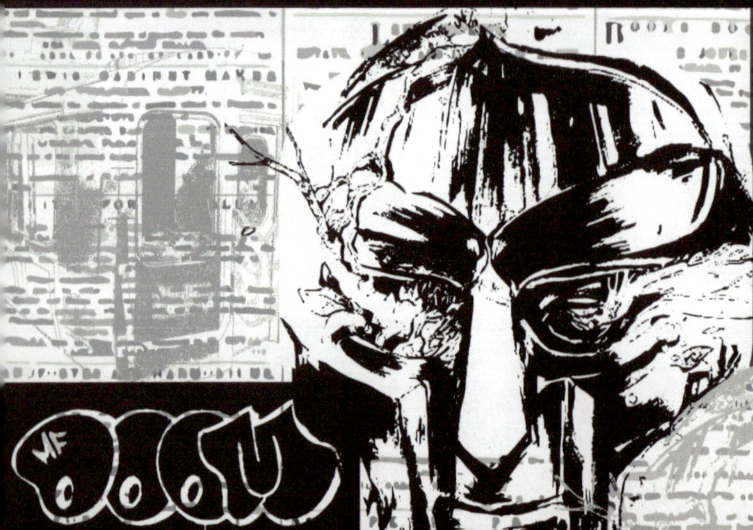

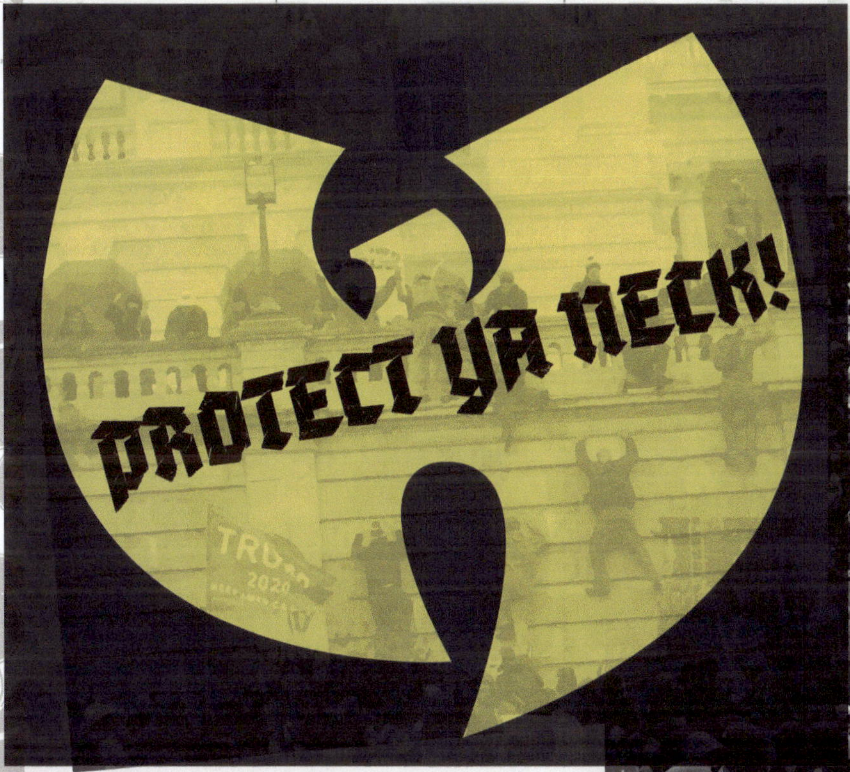

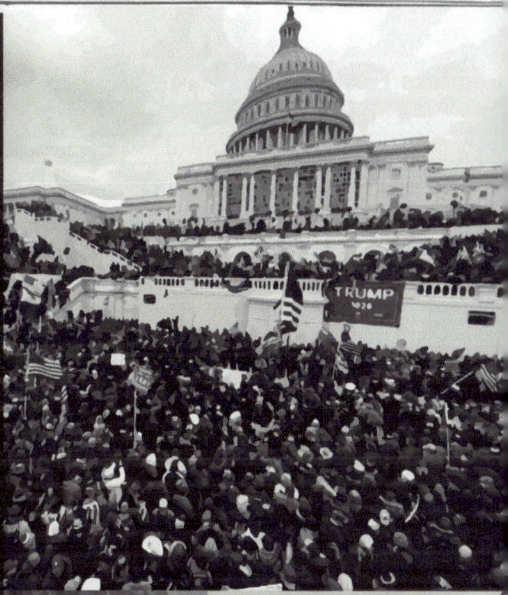

Permanent suspension of @realDonaldTrump

By Twitter Inc.
Friday, 8 January 2021

After close review of recent Tweets from the @realDonaldTrump account and the context around them — specifically how they are being received and interpreted on and off Twitter — we have permanently suspended the account due to the risk of further incitement of violence.

In the context of horrific events this week, we made it clear on Wednesday that additional violations of the Twitter Rules would potentially result in this very course of action. Our public interest framework exists to enable the public to hear from elected officials and world leaders directly. It is built on a principle that the people have a right to hold power to account in the open.

However, we made it clear going back years that these accounts are not above our rules entirely and cannot use Twitter to incite violence, among other things. We will continue to be transparent around our policies and their enforcement.

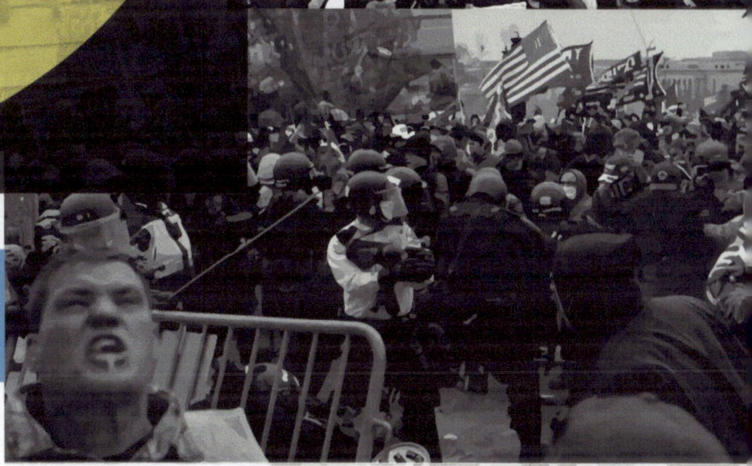

. (Joseph Prezioso / AFP / Getty)

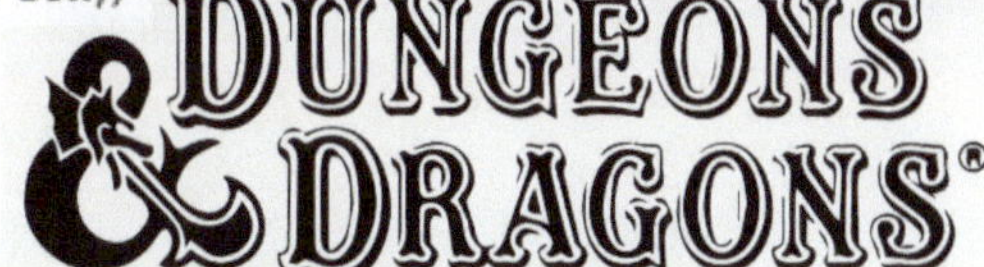

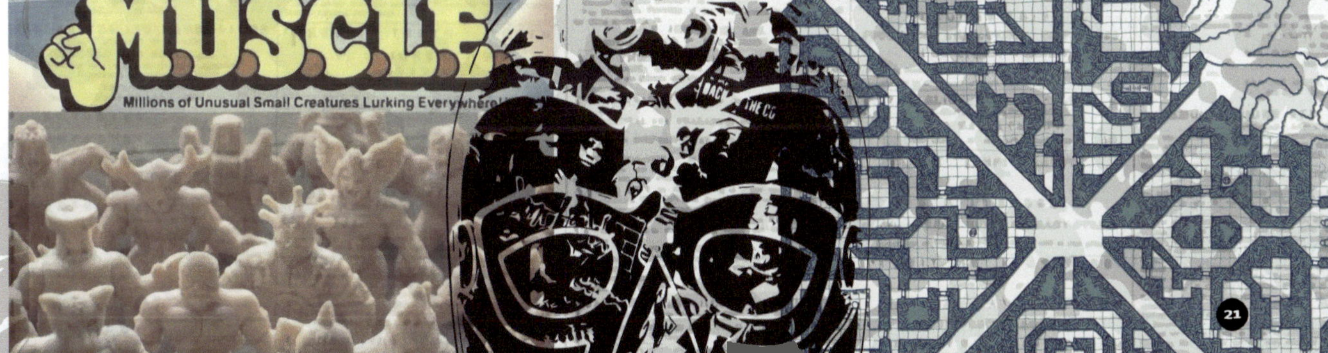

.GOV

Sign in.
Please check the box
for your reason for being here today.
Two forms of I.D.
And you must be able to present your
S.S. card or you won't be seen today.
Are you serious?
Yes.
Good because I brought it today.
You guys got me on this last time.
Waited 45 minutes and
then was turned away.
Yeah, that happens to a lot of people.
I bet it does.
I try to keep it short and sweet
so she doesn't turn me away
My ferris wheel spins
And no passengers are getting off
"We have one new rule we just
implemented this year
Ok
You must check your balls
here with me. What?
Is this part of Obama-care?
What about women?
Oh, they just leave their purses.
Damn, that's fucked.
No way I'm doing that!
It's part of the new policy.
So,if I want to be seen then…
Yes.
Wow!
I scoff but leave
my manhood in her hands.
I hope they give them a quick once over
before I get them back.
Save me a trip to the docs office.
So what am I here for again?
I look down at my options to check off?
Routine check up.

Fafsa application.
Entrance exam.
Ethnicity quiz?
Damn was it Latino? Hispanic.
or other.white hispanic?
Damn categories
are more fucked now than ever.
I don't feel white.
Why can't they get this shit straightened out.
We won this election.
They should just ask
where my parents were born?
I would probably still complain.
Back of the Yards and *Tepito*. Two hoods.
Back to my checklist.
Free Aids test
Art classes (small fee required)? Nice but no.
Unemployment application
Food stamps application
City parking tickets lay away
Missed connections
Casual encounters
Credit counseling
Marriage counseling
Dental work
Poetry prevention
& other
Of course I checked "other".
I gave the clipboard back to the girl
holding my nuts
Other people don't usually check this.
Well I've already been here
for all the other things.
So what is it you are looking for?
Knowledge.
Oh. that's gonna cost you.
Well I just want access
to some academic journals.
Those are even more expensive.
So what's it gonna cost me?
Your life.

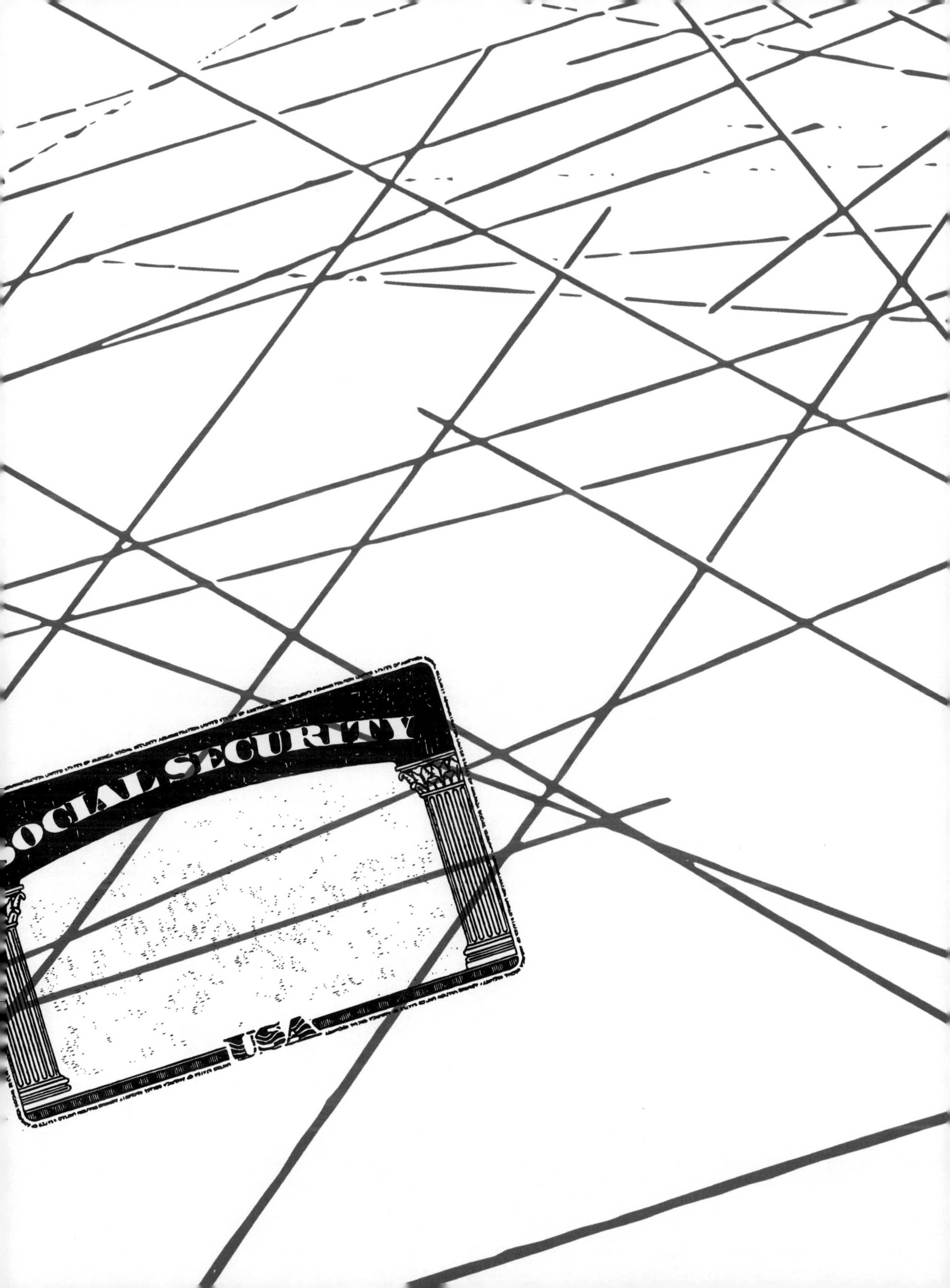
SOCIAL SECURITY
USA

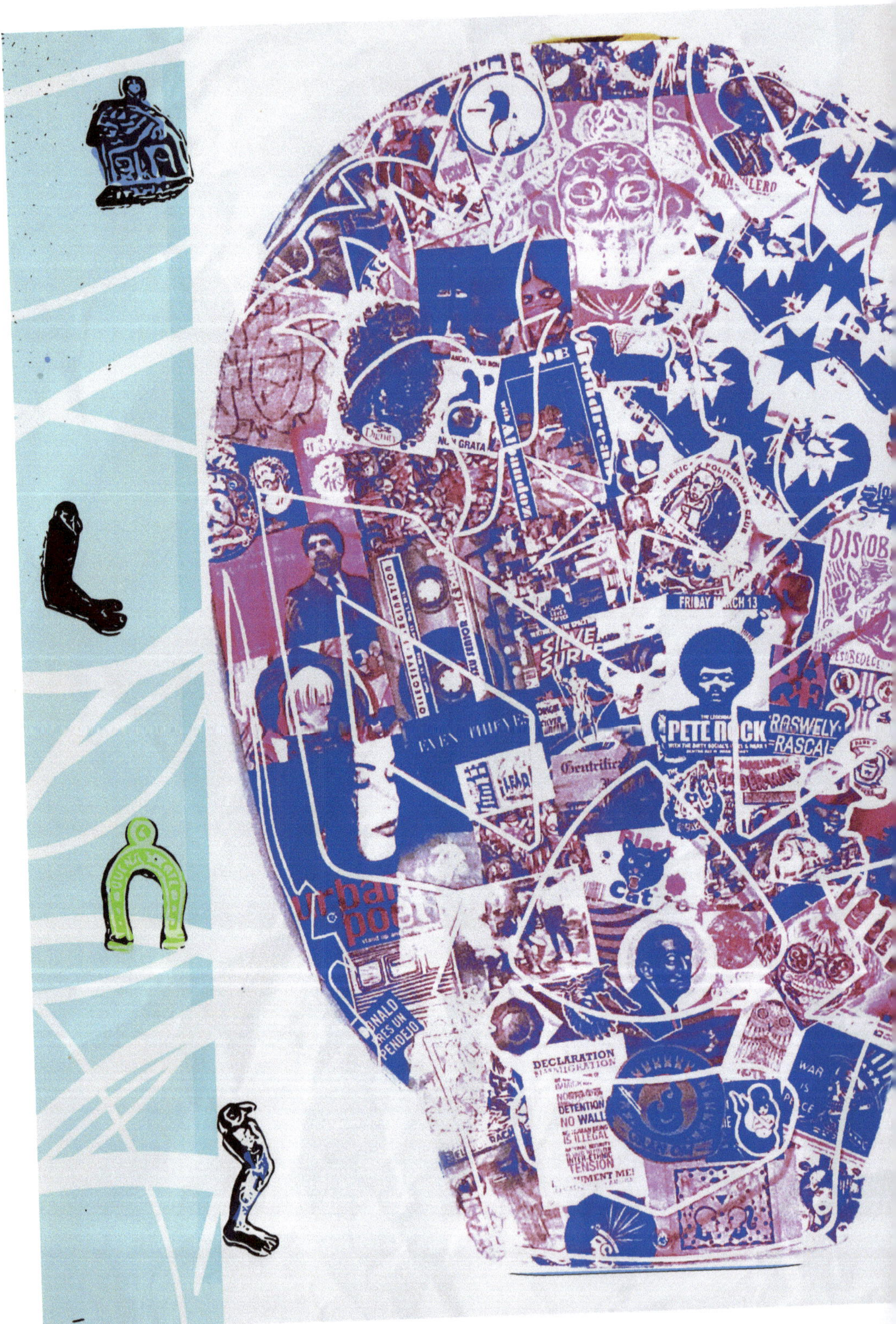

DR. MILAGROS

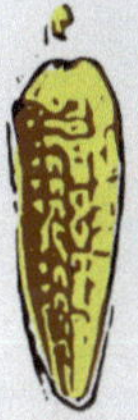

Pilsen pray for me
Teach me your wicked ways
Disassemble my insides
Abolish my gentry
Love my passion
Steal my color
Dream for me
Save me from myself
Set politics aside but vote
Believe in yourself
Dime que me quieres
Respetame! Destroy me
Delicious pero cuentame despues
Cuanto me quieres
Spit on me but open the door
Love my brownness
Heart my Blackness
Destroy my gamut
Lets see each others spectrum
Because you are ugly
But I love you
Mi querido Pilsen.

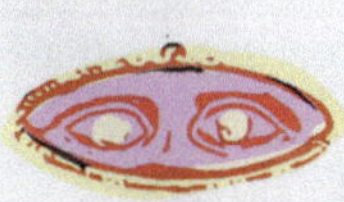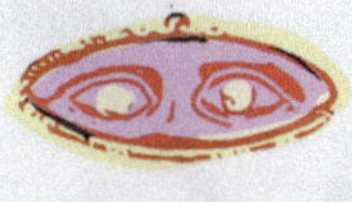
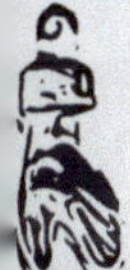

@1000MASKS

NOT JUST ANOTHER COLOR

Fun is the son
Of the color red
Twin of sin
And cousin of decision
You are beautiful
I met you at an exhibition
But I still knew
That blue was fool
That went to school
But still couldn't become
The color red
And if I kissed your tattoo
Would you still be red
And if red met green
Would it still be close to my birthday
Did you call or text
Or just protest my bed
Because my sheets
Were no longer white
And smelled like someone
Much more bright
Brilliant, beautiful
Dangerous, sharp like Excalibur
Blood and iron times twenty
And that color

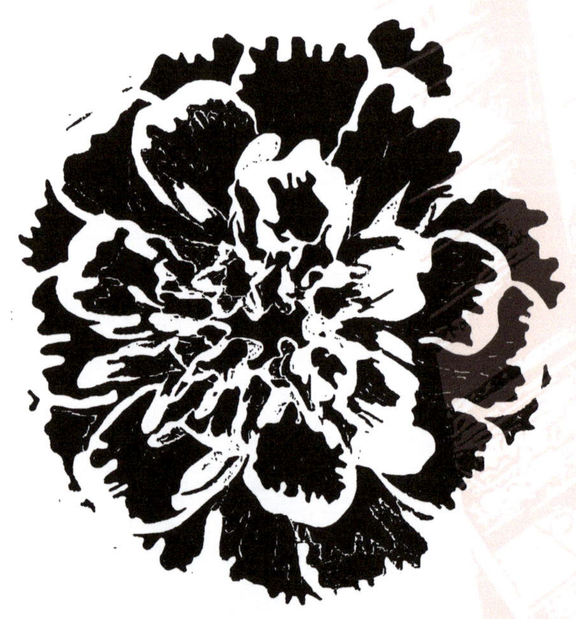

Lays, lies, lingers
Spit leftover
Applauding our many conquests
Other colors jealous of us
Could never be us
So they just whimper
And cover
Just as my room does
When you are not primary.
 Devastated like island
East that shares
Your bountiful spot
Round parts of you
My eyes trace
Until my lips taste
Your spectrum
My tantrum lasts
Just long enough
To make you squirm and smile
And see that pretty
Color red.

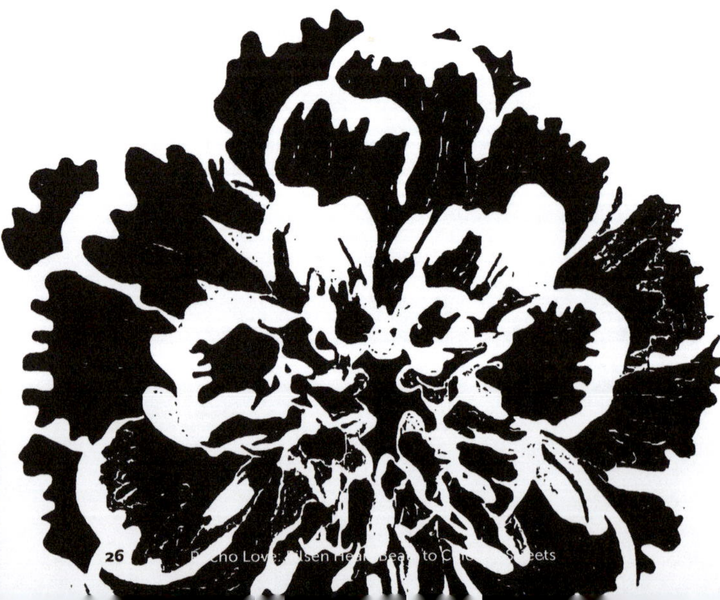

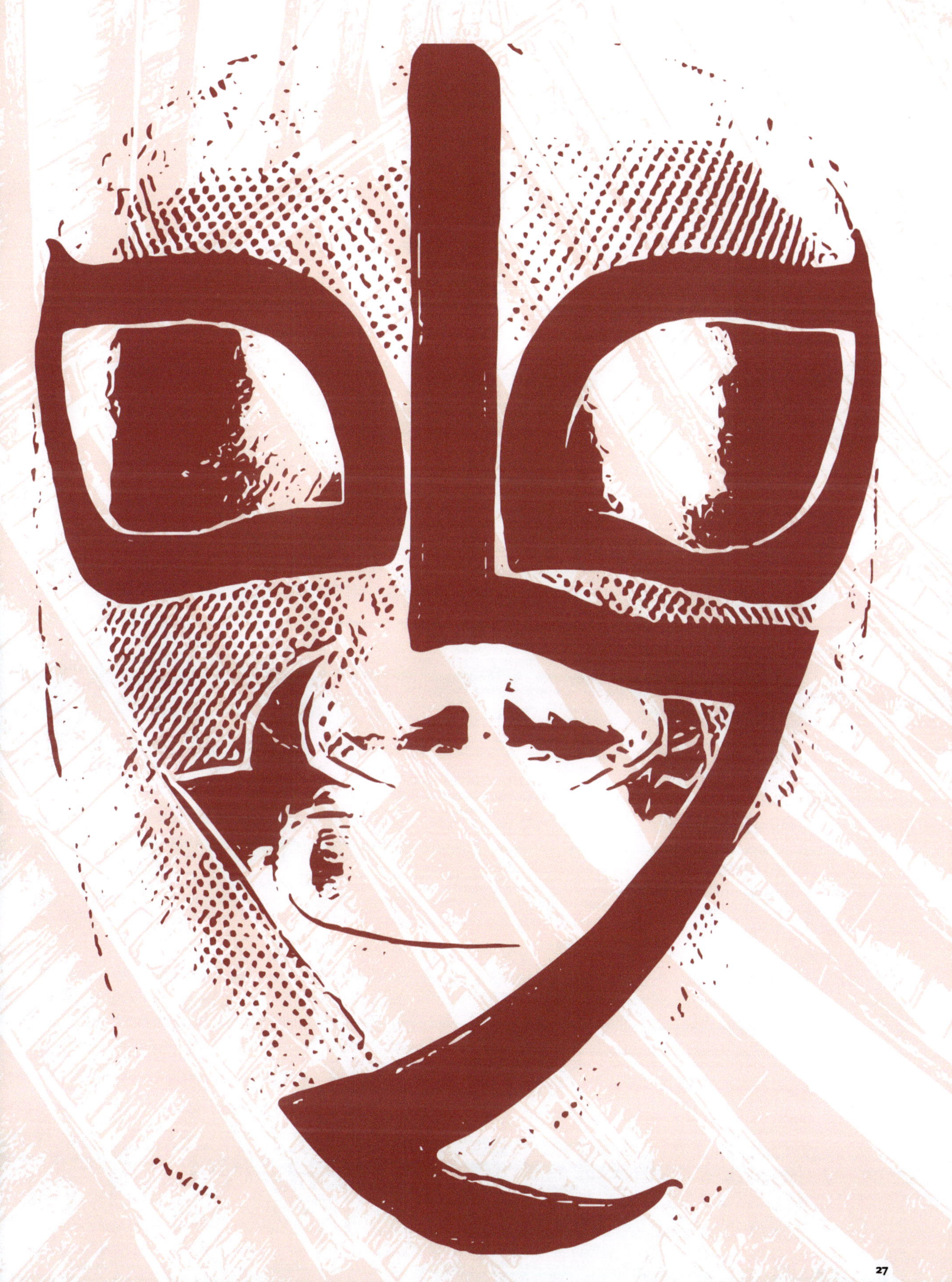

SLEEP

I want you to sleep with me
I want promises to be forgotten
And dreams to lay low beneath
Subtle silver sheets resting
Like left over change on a dresser
I want to sleep with you
I want to know your name
And your birthday wishes
Might not ever come true
I want to sleep with you
I want to lick your silent lips
And whispers softly ask
What is love? I don't know
I want to hold you
Like a handle does a mug
I want to sleep with you
I want worries to hide
Like the mango sun sleeps
Even if it's just the night
I want to trust those lies
That light your beauty
Plays with and manipulates
Like Toys R Us silly putty
I wanted for my birthday
To sleep with you
I want the heat in our hearts
To meet like attracted CTA eyes
On the five-fifteen *tren*
Except not in vain
Because they are sure to meet
Again
To sleep with you
I want your fiery curls
To wake up the passion that's inside
And remember how it's
always good in the movies
Sex is what I want,
Maybe, I need to make love to you
No, I want to sleep with you.
But then again
When have you ever given me
What I wanted.

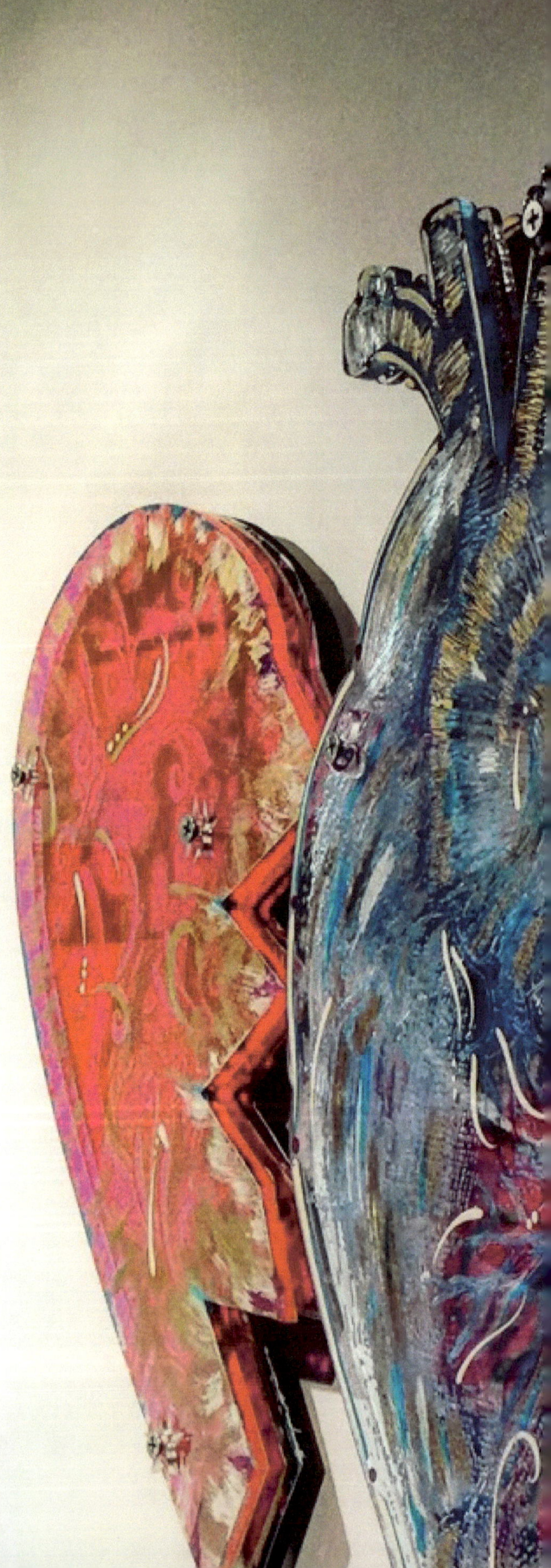

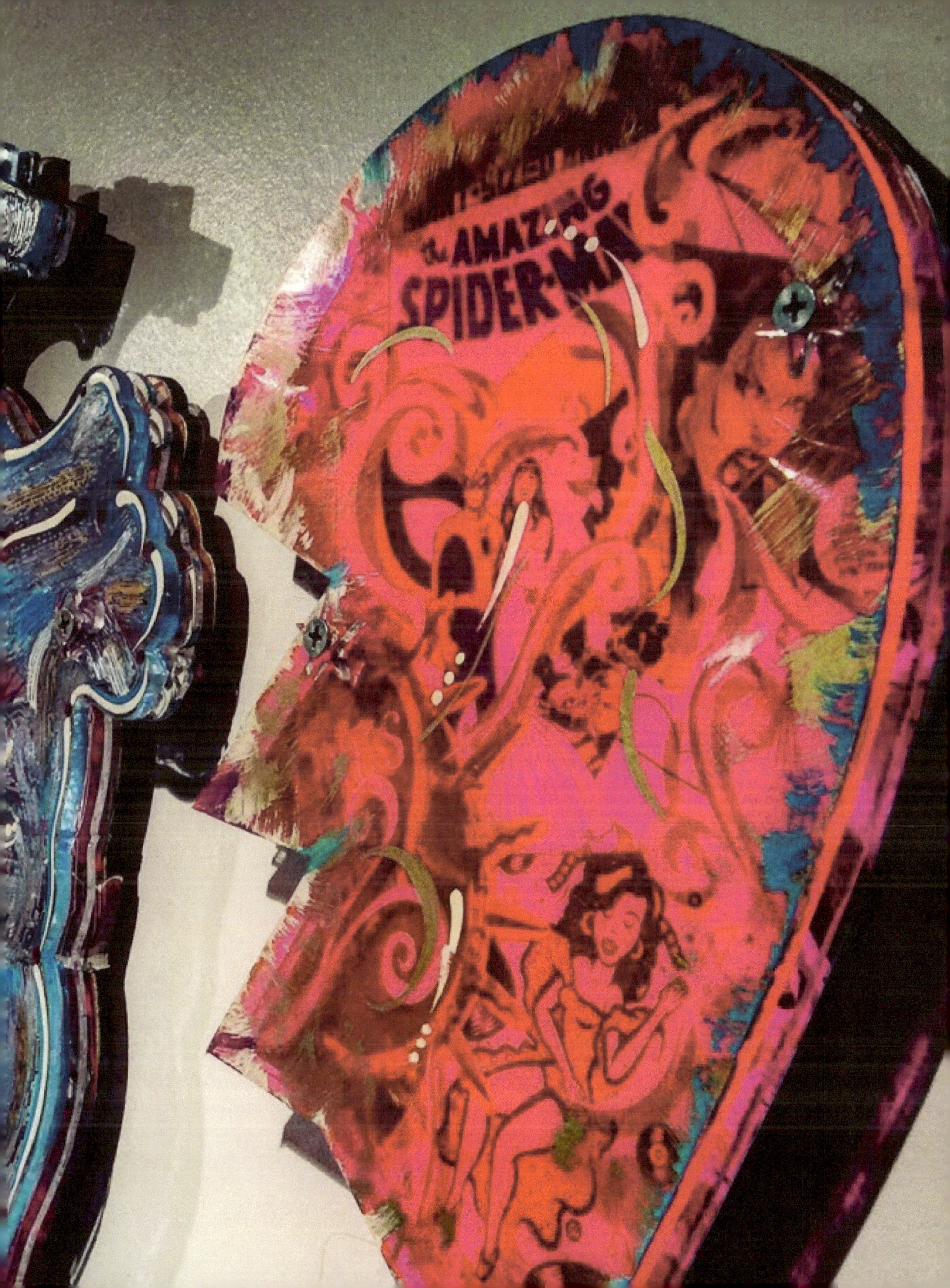
THE AMAZING
SPIDER-MAN

HARDLY

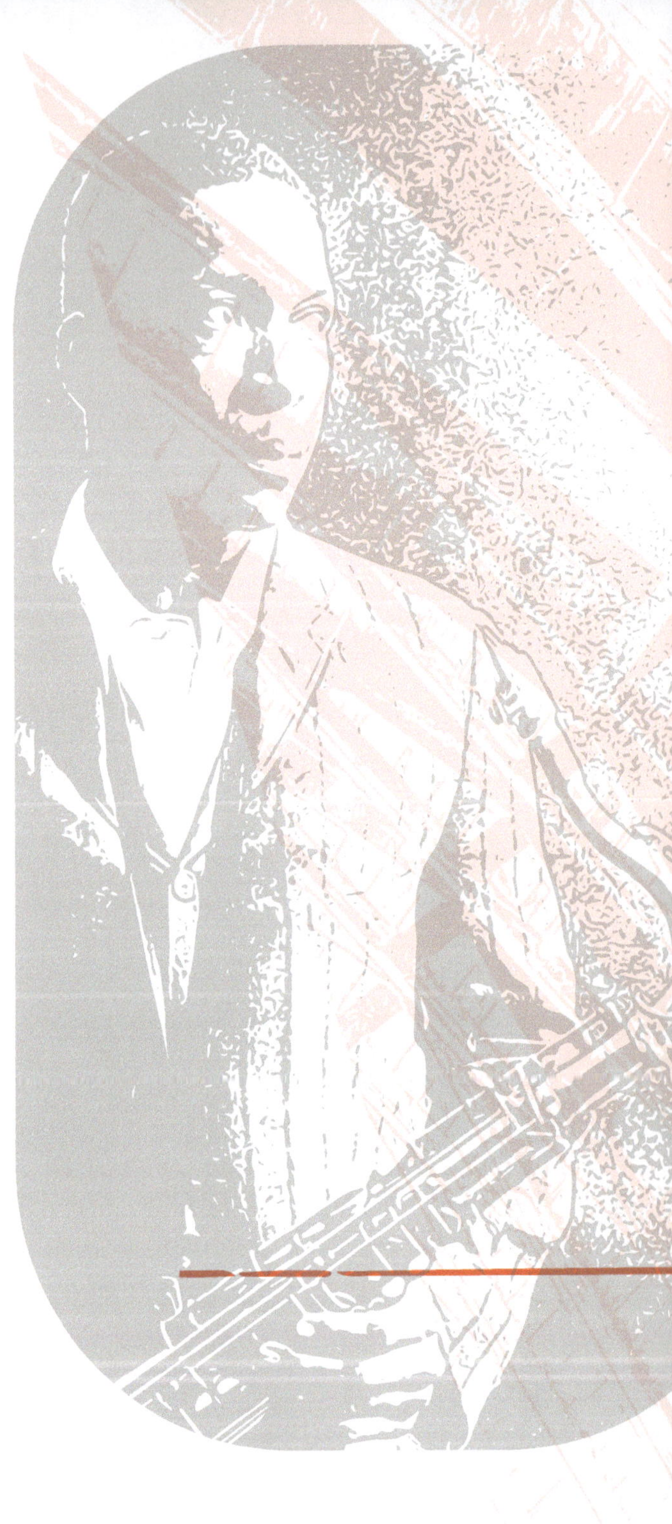

Hard and heartbroken
A love supreme plays
I could write a good poem
about that but I'm busy
Hard and heartbroken
I need to break this sentence of solace
Maybe I go in search of three dollar hoes
At the two dollar spot
But will you be there?
Hard
Days like nights
Tonight make me forget
Tomorrow
Deliver me cheap
like Madds Pizza at midnight
Because I choose to be
Broke, broken
Heartbroken
My jaguar died a heinous Chicago death
Flooded in a south side basement
Don't act like you do not know
Or that it hasn't happened to you
Hardly
Hard
Heart
Distances become seconds
When you say yes, yes, yes
Nobody plays me better
Or softens my sky
So sweet
Smooth
Savory like Dillabeats
Hard, heart
Broken
Disturbed like 4 a.m.
shout outs via S.M.S
And by then someone
else has my attention
A love supreme plays
I could write a good poem about that.

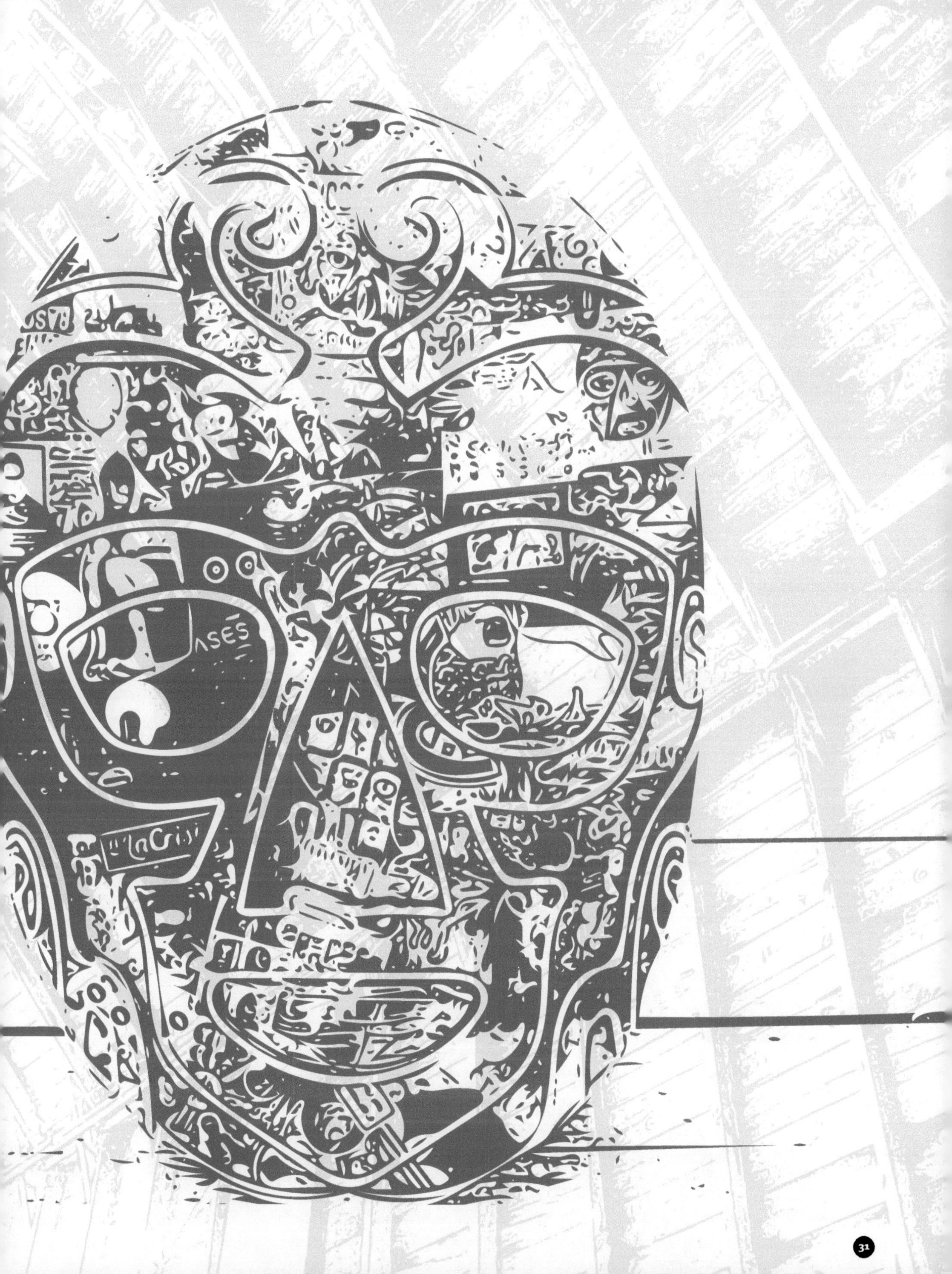

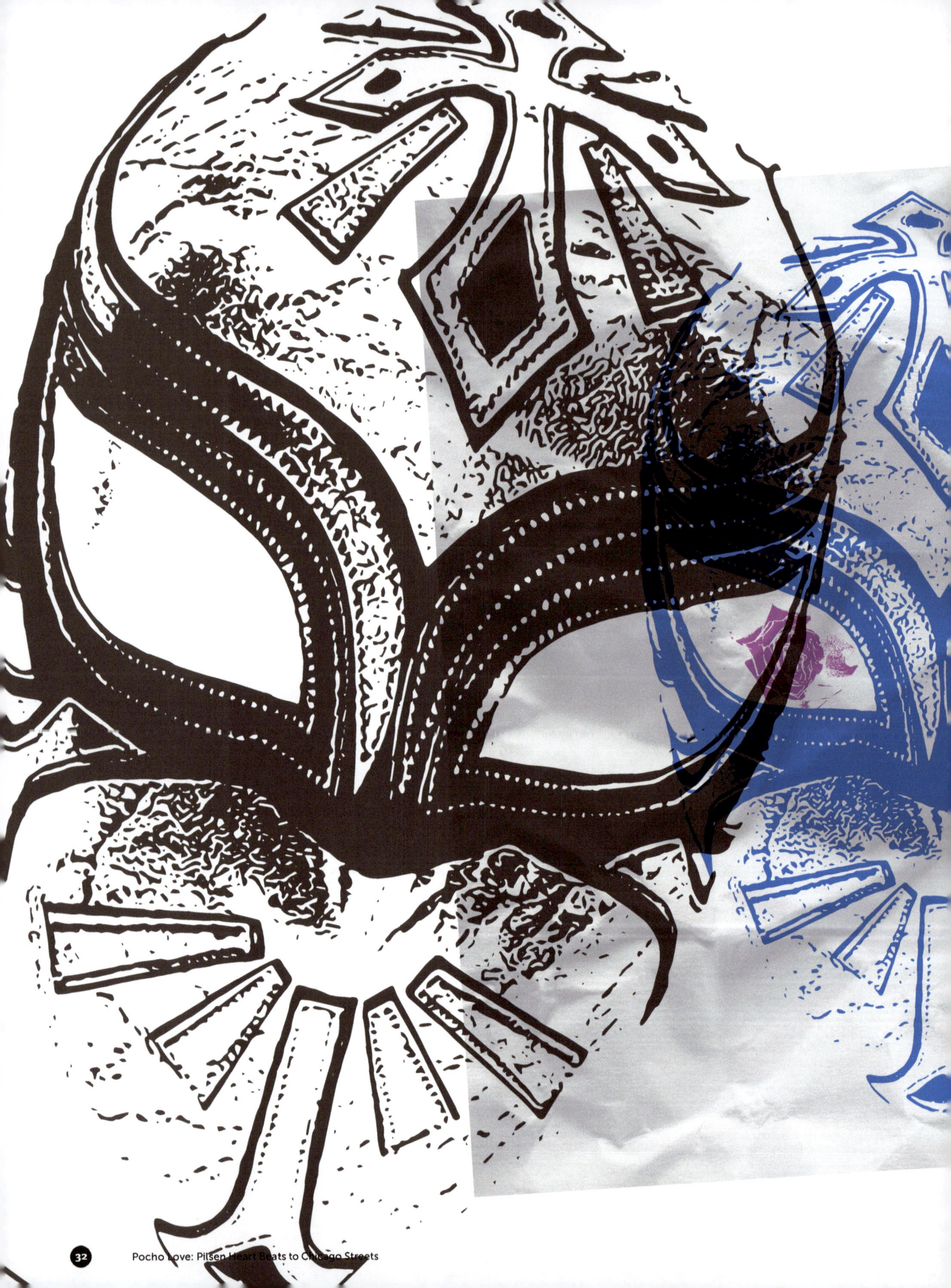

  Pocho Love: Pilsen Heart Beats to Chicago Streets

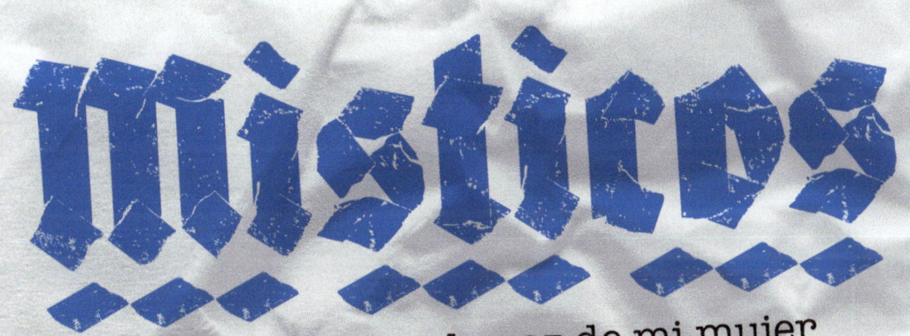

Misticos

Me desperté ayer con la voz de mi mujer
preguntándome donde ir a comprar carnitas
y le dije que fuera a la cuarta dimensión.
Que trajera nopalitos ricos hechos por diablitos
y comprara aguacates medios verdes
para hacer una salsa para los ciudadanos.
Desperté ayer con el miedo del mundo y recé
por primera vez en años y me comí media
docena de tortillas con la cena.
Desperté ayer con el chisme del Face y pensé
porque es que nos fusilamos tan facil.
Desperté ayer con ganas de aprender Inglish
para poder acabar mis poemas chafas.
Desperté ayer con rosas en mis ojos porque así
los dejaste anteayer.
Desperté ayer con recuerdos de las luchas y de mi
abuelo que ahora vive en los montes de Zacatecas
vigilando las tunas rojas llenas de tristeza.

Desperté ayer con fuego en la lengua y compartí
mi plan de ir a votar. Desperté ayer...   @1000MASKS

DRIPS

Sin and cinnamon
Say good morning
Before coffee envelops
Your skin perfume
Your curves speak
Only of previous
Dimpled lakes
And take me to places
Ive only dreamt of
I cough only because you
Breath and I am
Your reflection
drips hips sips
Thick with bliss
Baked because
Chicago sweats in September
I explore more so
You can be on repeat
Rolodex of letting go
Drips hips sips
A little more
Taste my adornment
So we can sync
Before we melt
Into our mistakes
Our 4th dimension
That holds us even without
Rings or knowing each others
Passwords
Or accounts
Or fears or dares
To keep going on
Drips hips sips
More and again
So we destroy
Each other equally
And completely before
The sun tickles your button nose
And our lips
Say hello again

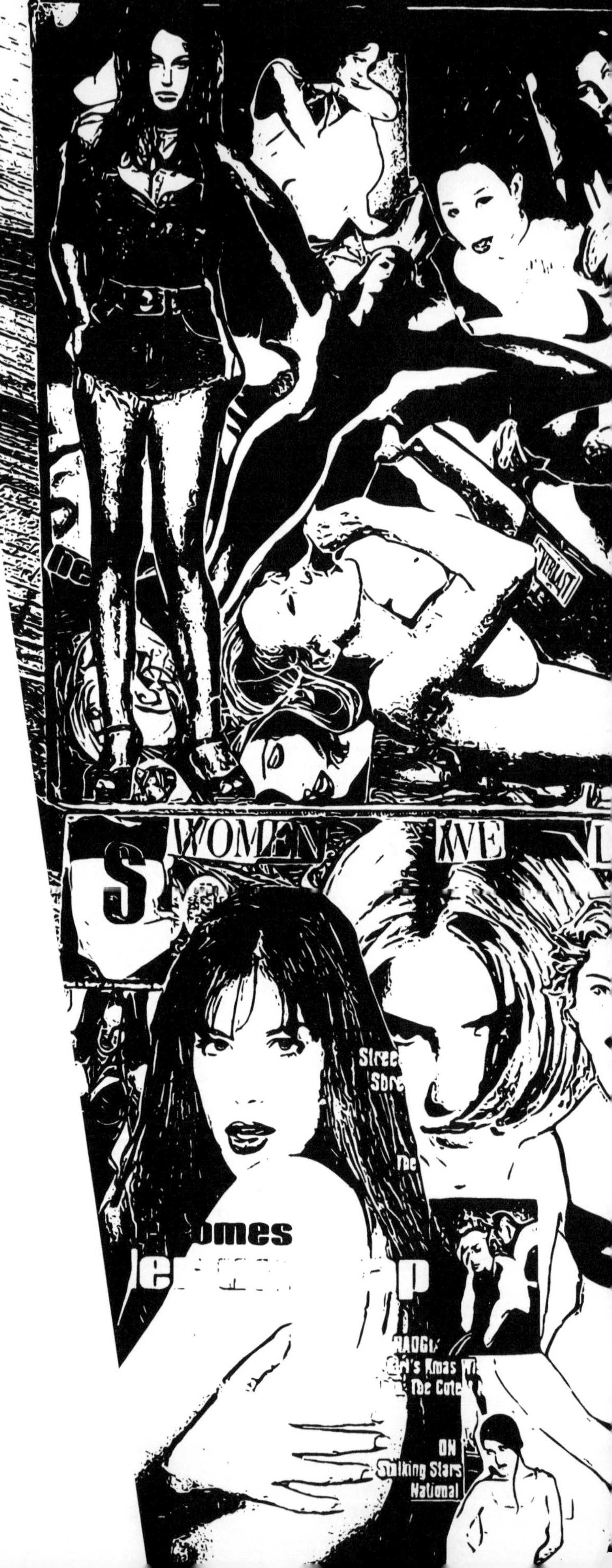

NOUVEAU CHOLA

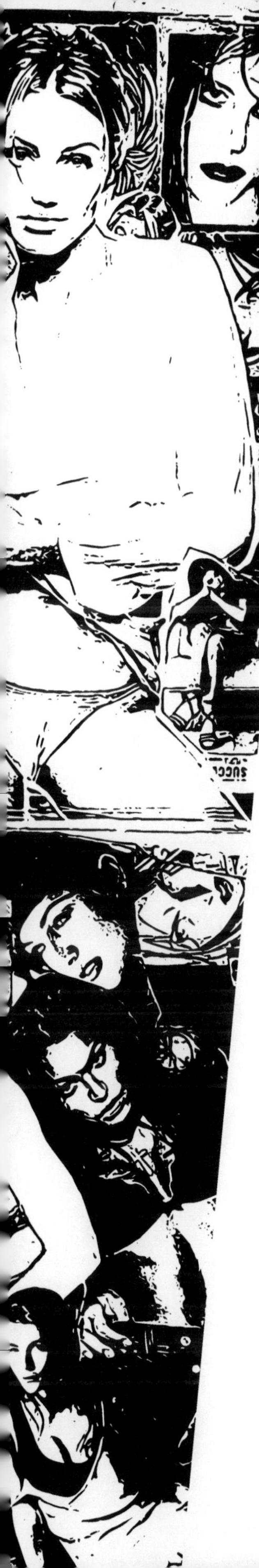

Nouveau Chola
No te conozco
Pero déjame entrar
Pestañas negras
Tipped and delightful
Tus ojos me conocen
Porque soñé con ellos
Wildstyle black hair
Con coraje
Salvaje
Como novelas
De Univisión
We enter only
so we can say
Goodbye
Daily
Notes we seed so
We don't starve
Tomorrow
I will say hello
So its not so awkward
Nouveau chola
Your fit finds
Designer vintage
Tees that make you
Feel comfortable enough
to make your body invisible.
But I still notice

Your reflection in all
Windows as I walk past
Nosy neighbors
And busy gangways
And think about how
you also
Walk these streets
And they get jealous
Of your lips
With just enough
Lipstick to make me sweat
With nervous
Intention
Nouveau Chola
Dickies and button downs
Stand between us
Discos y delicias
Palabras y paletas
De mango lechosas
And melting melting melting
Like time when
I remember
Que ni te conozco
Y ni se tu nombre
Nouveau Chola
Nos vemos mañana.

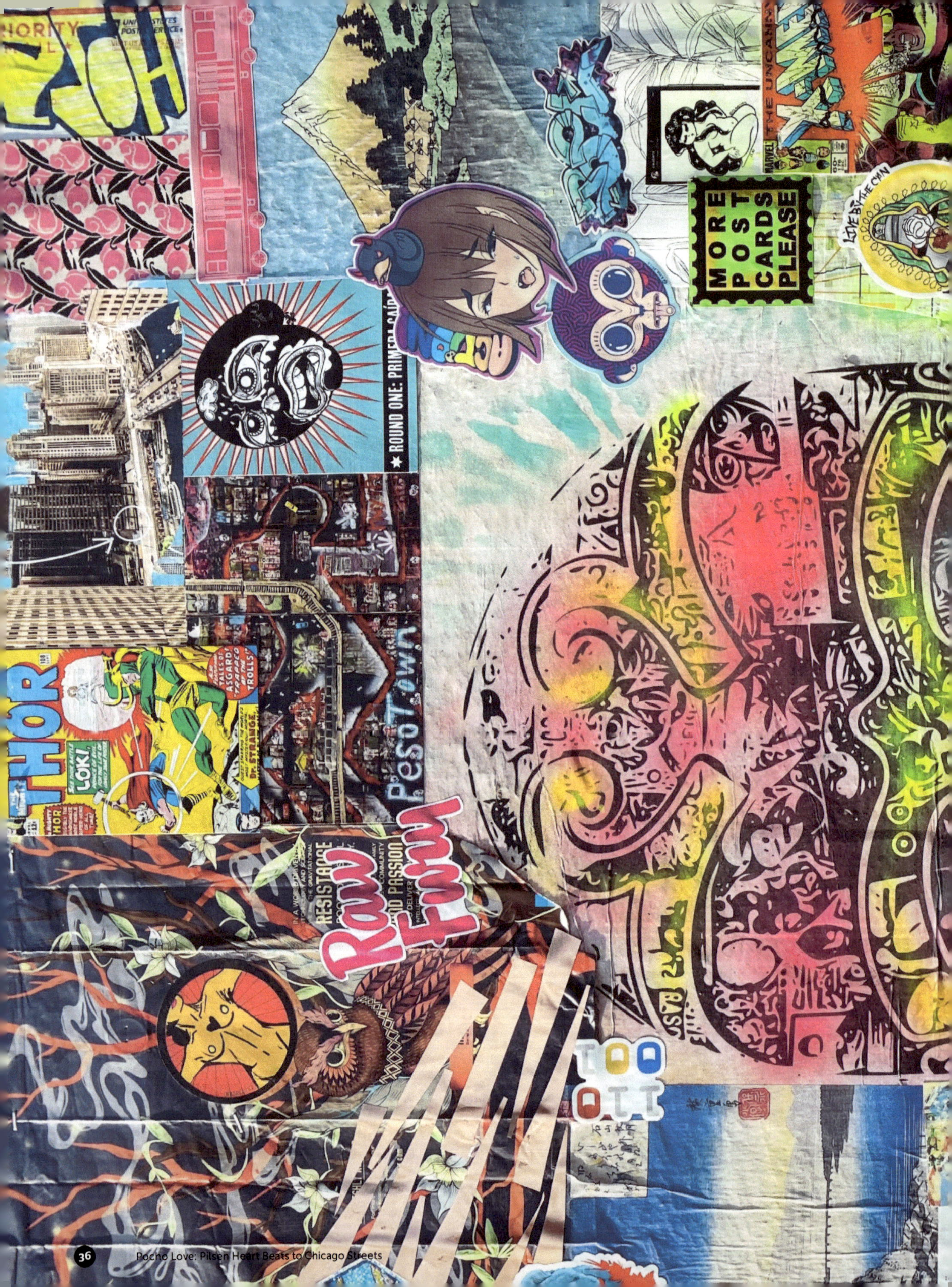

MORE POST CARDS PLEASE
THOR
LOKI
Dr. STRANGE
Raw Fun
PesoTown
ROUND ONE: PRIMERA CAIDA
THE UNICARD

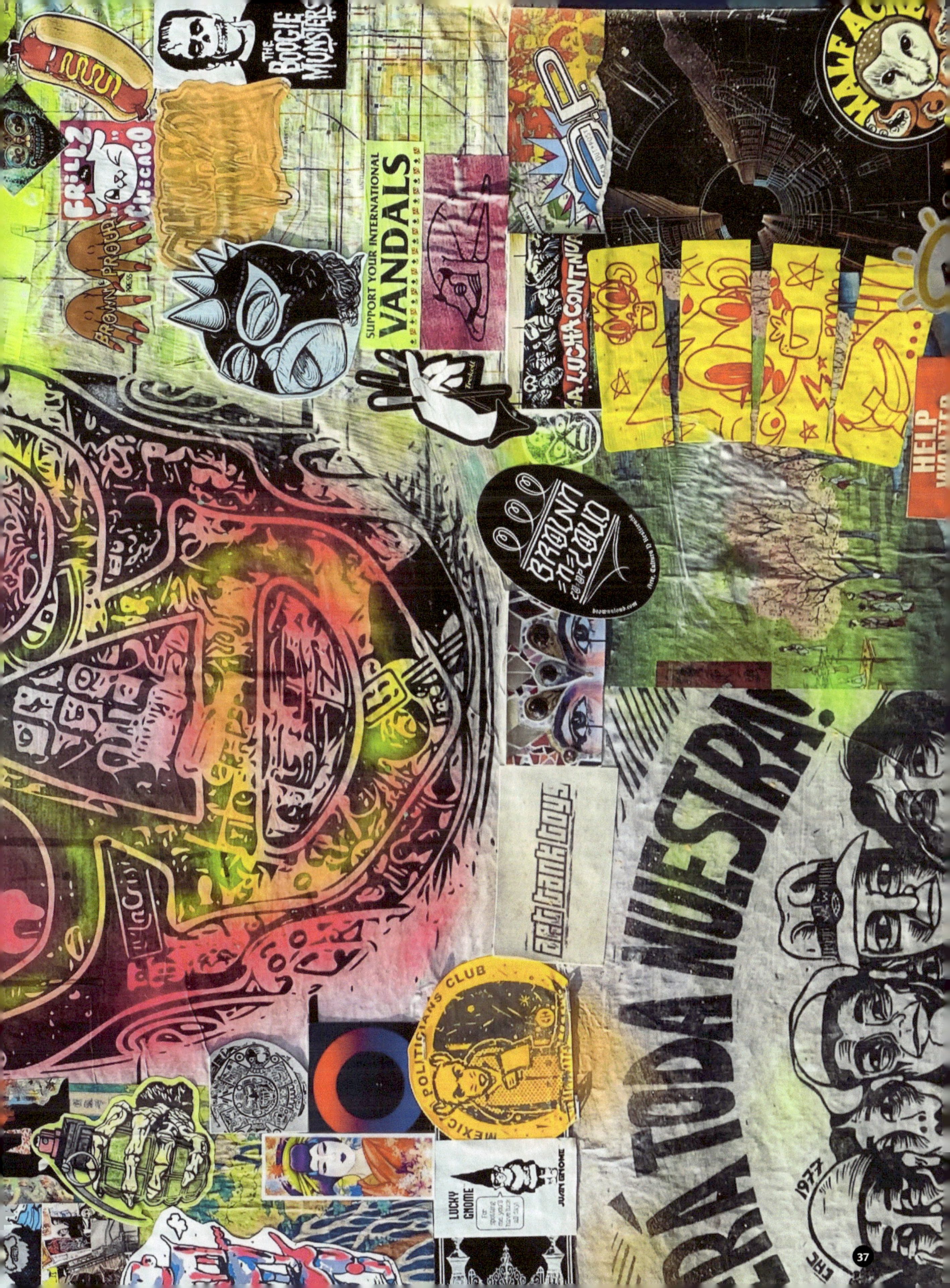

THE BOOGIE MUNSTERS
MALFACRE
D.I.P.
BROWN PROUD CHICAGO
FRILLZ
SUPPORT YOUR INTERNATIONAL VANDALS
LA LUCHA CONTINUA
HELP WANTED
BROWN-N-CLOUD
browncloud.com
POLITICIANS CLUB
MEXIC
LUCKY GNOME
JUAN GNOME
ERA TODA NUESTRA
1977
ERIC

Grounds wake
& you tremble beside me
entertained by the destruction
Our palms sway
Leafy promise & sandy
Nothing
Tempts me more
and brings me rage
as you nibble my sanity
Desparate to escape
our inseparability.
Not worthy, our beach
is untouched
Our city crumbles
Our politicians stuck
& sinking, sinking
Feelings numb
As we embrace

Quarantined like dreams
Safe but disintigrating
Our cure is each other
As we transform together

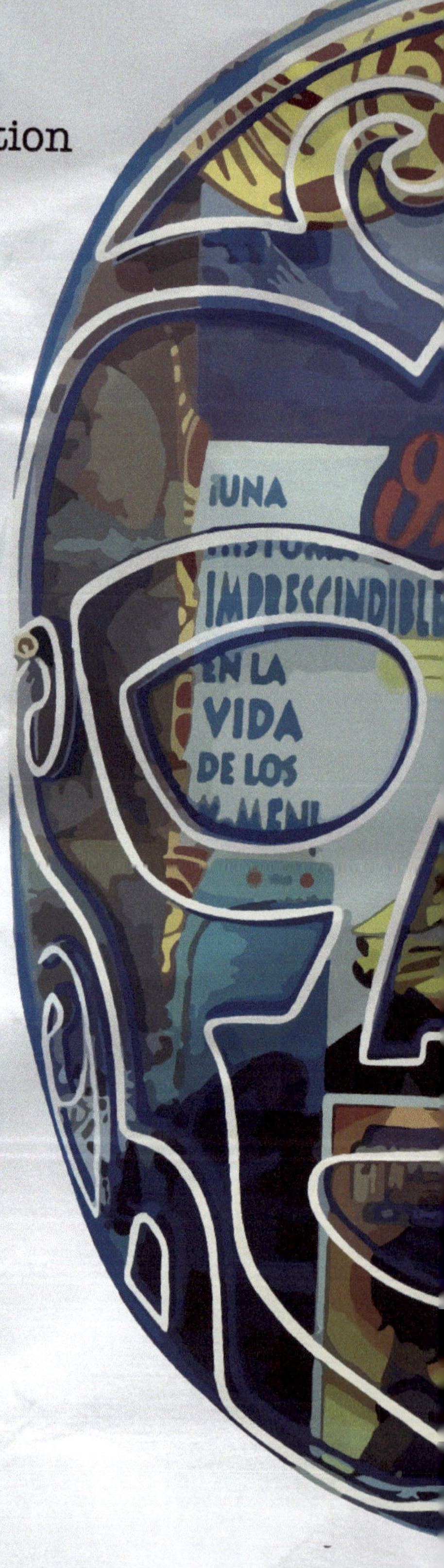

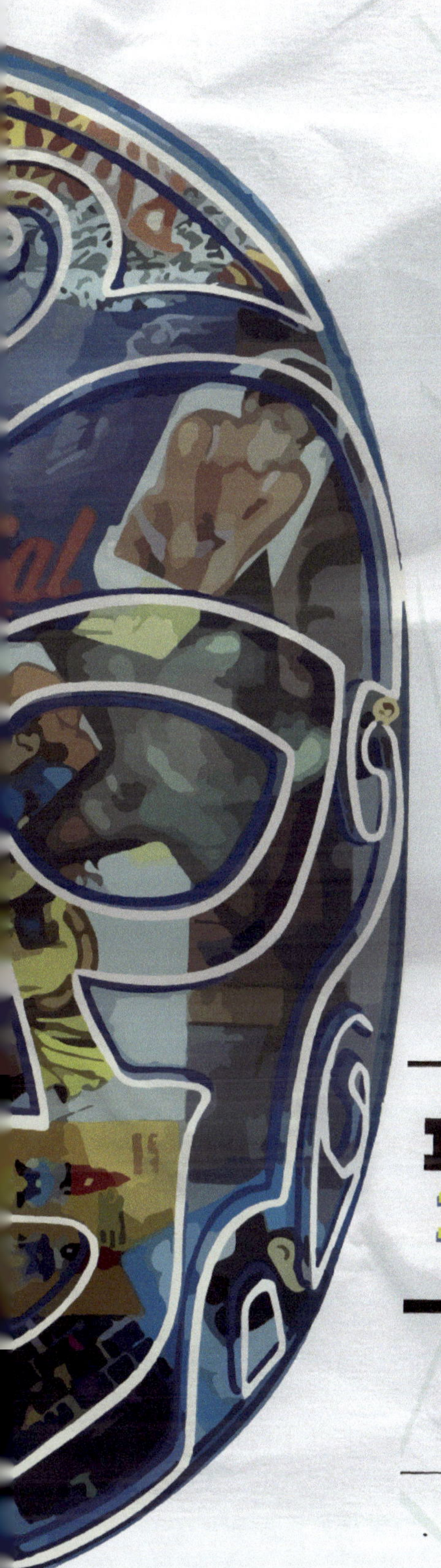

Lightning strikes
Twice on occasion
Thunder claps
over and over till we
distance like covid
Masks
Like soft blues notes
We tie around each other
Perfect knots
Glorietas en ciudades
Distantes Distant
So I pull you closer
So you can
See me
Madre Michigan
Can't you see
your waves are
drowning us all.

HURACAN RAMIREZ

@1000MASKS

THE OTHER STORY
WORLDWIDE
Cypress Hill
EL MALIGNO

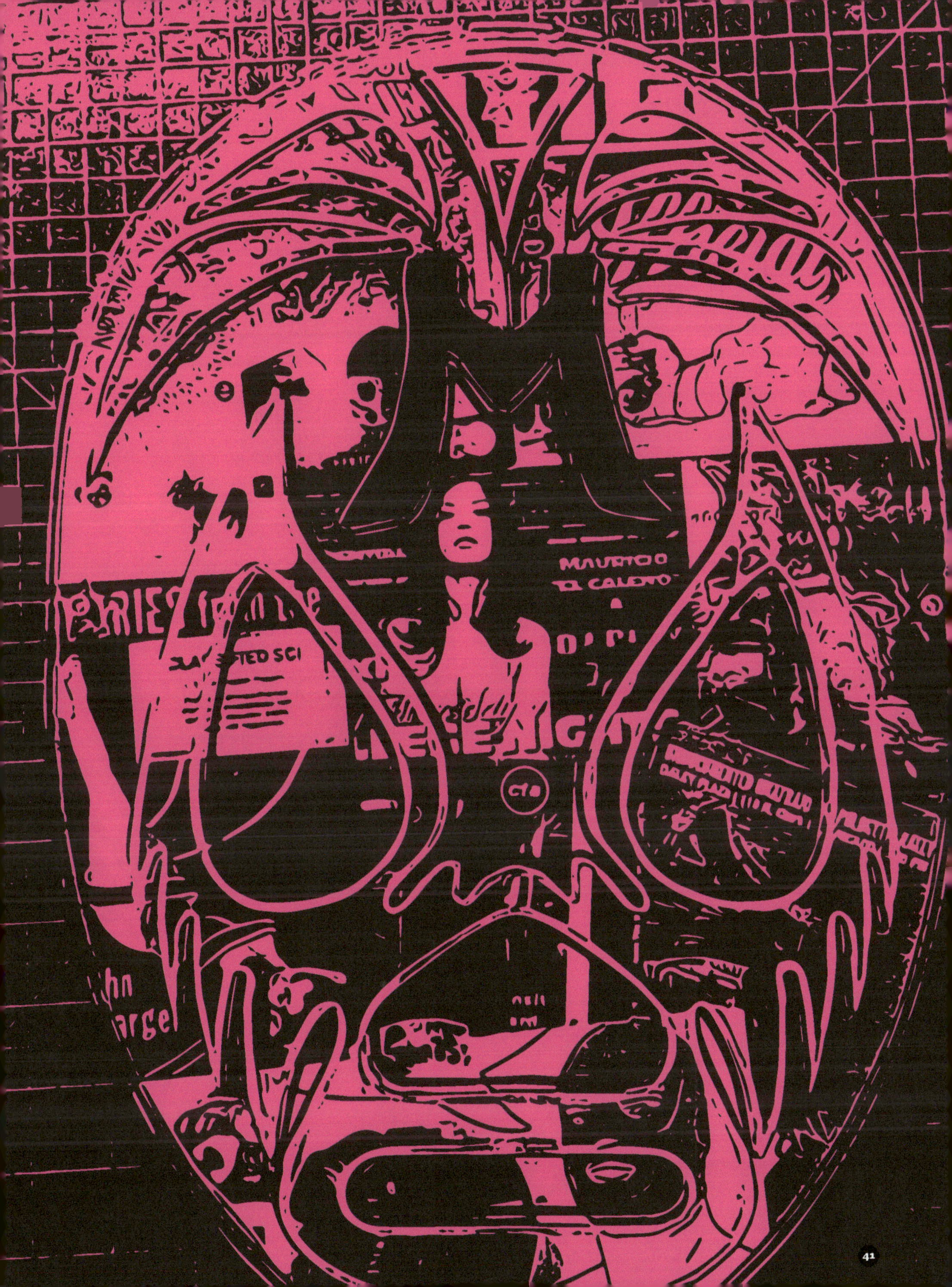
PRIE
TED SCI
MAURIZIO
DI CALENO
hn
rgel

GIRLS THAT GOT AWAY

Perfect incantation
Romantic ejaculation
Words without brains
Pero con huevos
"Would you like to have
breakfast with me?"
Simple so you smiled
But I haven't said anything yet
You smell good so I get closer
You shy away but your lashes look over
Deserted shoulder
Sizzling *porque Dios*
Played with coffee
When you were made
Flowers died of jealousy
You look the type so I touch your elbow
Really kinky, but you like it
Te das la media vuelta
And now I get a good look
Mango mami
Dulce de durazno
Dile que la quieres
Say something
The girls that got away
because I didn't say
"Hello". "*Hola*"
"What are you drinking?"
"Is that your man"
"Can I buy you a drink?"
"Is that your friend?"
"Are you drunk?"
"Yes, Gregorio is too old!"
"Let's go out sometime"
"I really like you"
"Damn you are fine!"
"I'm crazy about you!"
"Weeds on Dayton, Weeds on T.V., or weed?
"Let's fuck!"

"Stay with me tonight!"
"My hyperbole is in love
with your simile!"
"Live with me"
Don't get ahead of yourself
You stare right at me
Ojos borrachos
But I still want to
do backstrokes in them
You have not forgotten
I drink gin
Cantinera flirts
So you pay more attention
And tell me your name
I repeat it in my head
three times so I don't forget
But I do anyway
Pero nunca esas curvas
Never those curves
In two languages
Because I'm serious about this
momentary
Beat, Beat, Beat, Skip
Beat, Love, Lust, Love
Mojitos
Because you just ordered one
And you let me taste your lips
On your straw
And you invite me
Into your life
Too easy,
so I'm on to
la proxima.

EL PASO

Did I forget to dream last night
Or was it all your fault?
And if it was were you aware
Of what you were doing
Cuantas promesas
Dejaron escapar tus pestañas
La noche que me fuí y porqué
Es que nunca dormí tan atento
Con un labio sobre algodón
Un ojo escondido detrás de tu cuello
Y una mano debajo tu pecho
Respetando el derecho de tu corazón
Encadenado pero libre por primera vez
Floating on the winds whisper while
Being nestled in the clouds cradle
We didn't need a sheet
but we grabbed one anyway
Covering each other with our eyes
Or better yet, holding on
To something we haven't had
Together we feared the alarm clock radio
And as I would have done
You put it to sleep when it woke up
Con labios que daban pasos delicados
 Y manos contentos en abrazo
Aprendí cómo es que se debe amar
Cabello negro suelto
Raspando mis cachetes
Por que así de cerca quisiste estar
Generosa regalando besos
Que decías que no tenías
Lovable potential peeking and leaving
Only to return again
To your round room
Round because nothing outside
seemed to matter
As much as your touch
And your decaffeinated eyes
Yes, I am addicted
No, you don't have to tell me

That you love me
Because I felt it
Even before you
tried to use it
To say goodbye
Before the rush
Before the passion
Before you fell on me
Like raindrops
rushing to explode
On every friendly surface
Before I cared
Before you dared
Before I slept
Before we wept
Before Evas fashioned
Before the army stole you
Before I got a chance
to hold you
Before the roses
Before O'Hare International
Before the excuses
And after the excuses
Before fear of each other
Before we danced together
And shared a coke
Before we ever laughed
at the same thing
Before el paso
And after Korea
Before I shared
Before I forgot to dream
I learned to love.

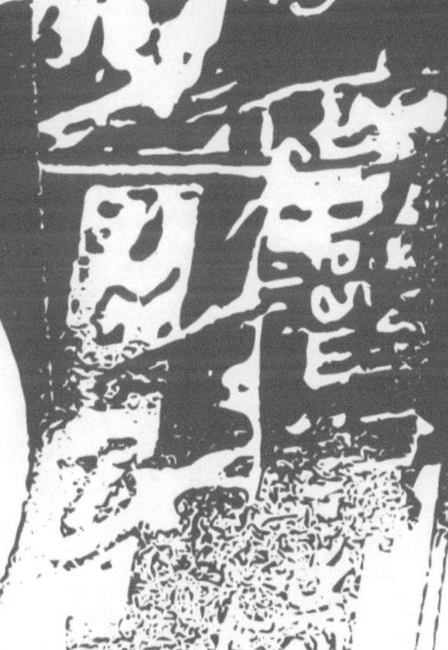

BROWN
=N= LOUD
co-op
brownnloud.com
Arte, Cultura N Resistencia
@teresamagart
NCHE
RONA
Lucky Gnome
I have the power!
LUNA

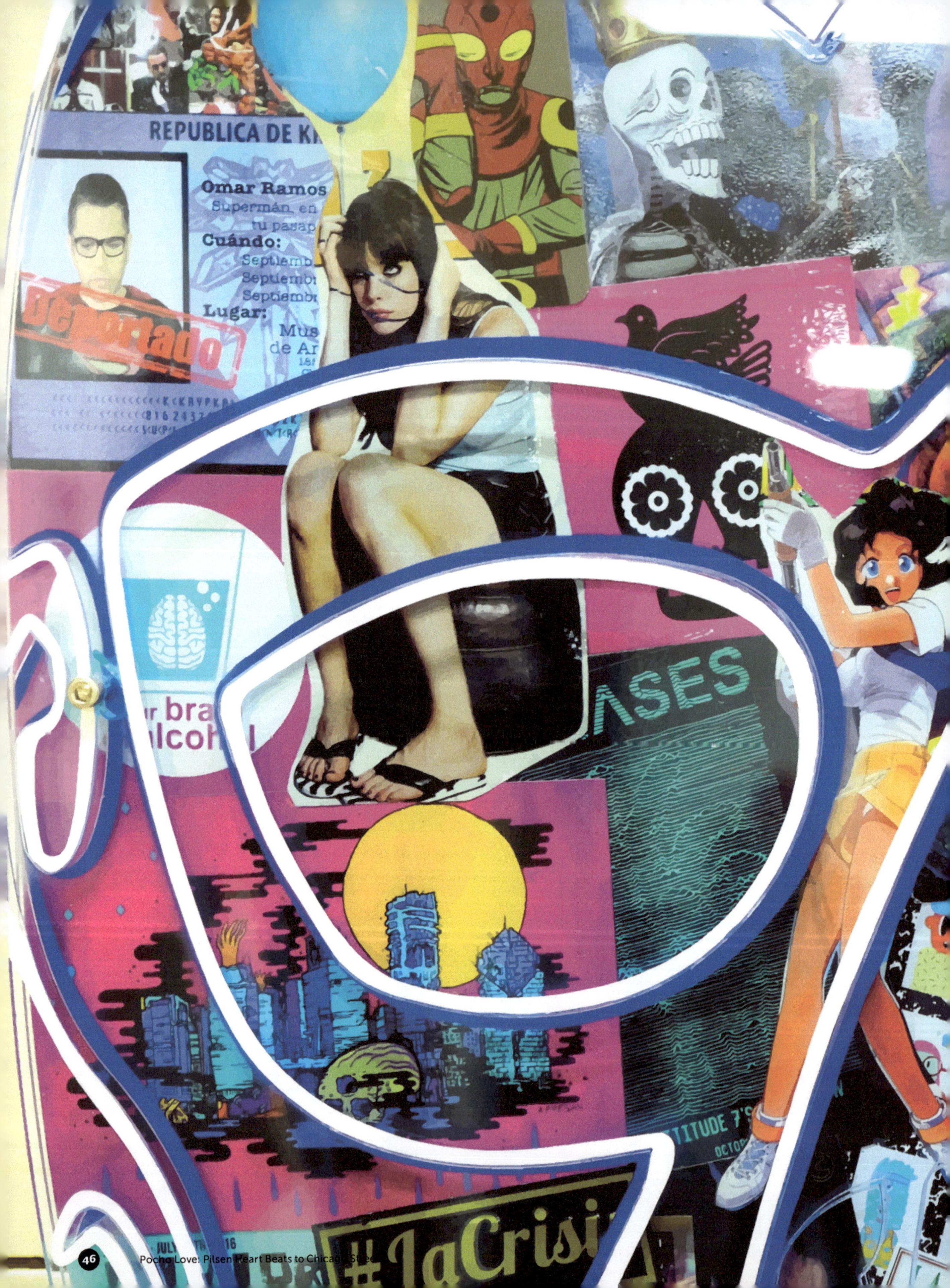

REPUBLICA DE KR
Omar Ramos
Supermán, en
tu pasap
Cuándo:
Septiemb
Septiembr
Septiembr
Lugar:
Mus
de Ar
ASES
#LaCrisi

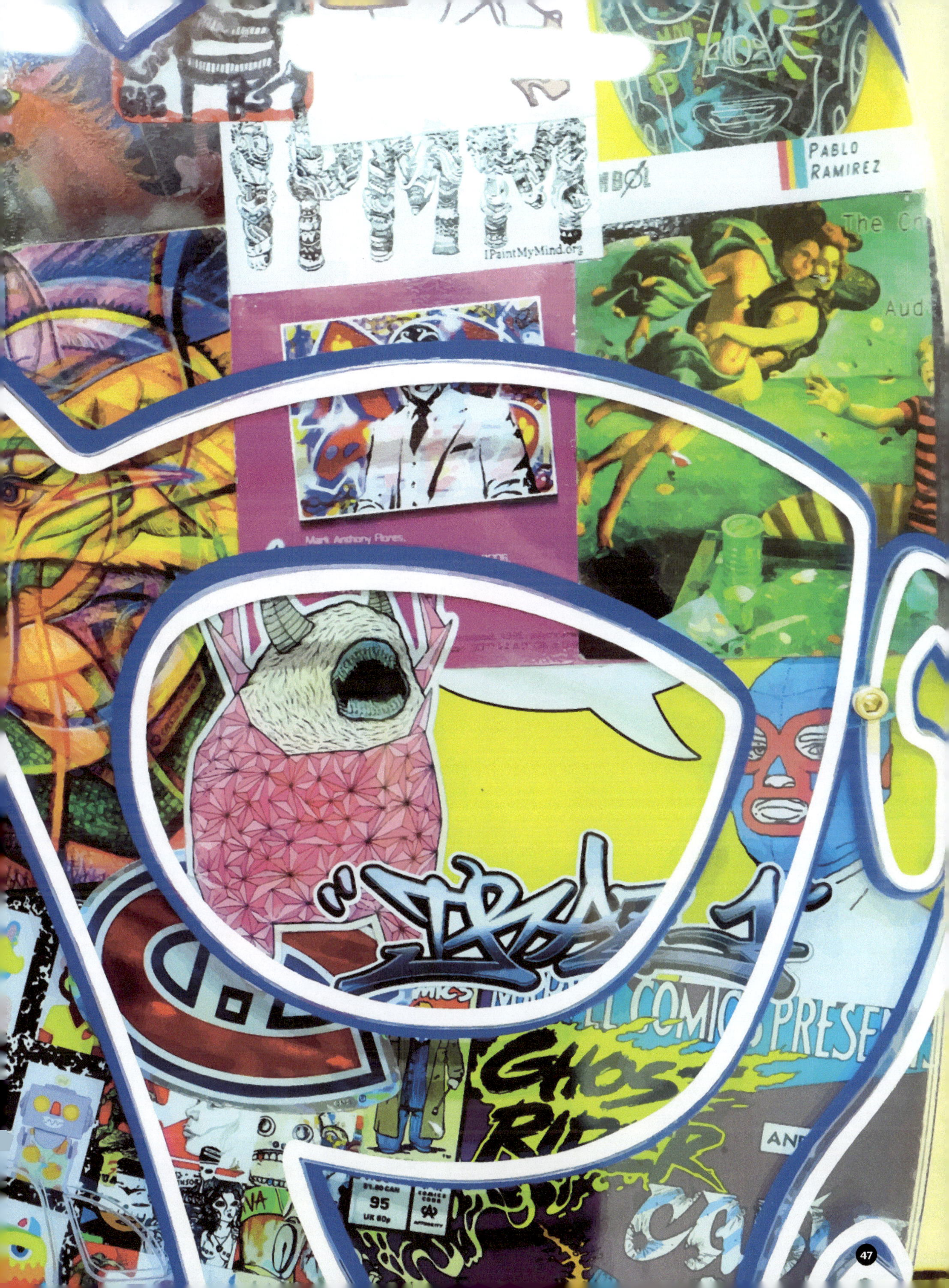
IPaintMyMind.org
PABLO RAMIREZ
Mark Anthony Flores.
The C
Aud
COMIC PRESE
GHOS
RI
AN
95
UK 80p

EVE

It's election eve
And I don't give a fuck!
How many more signs
Can I ignore
Really?
Why do you wait till midnight
to put your name on my corner?
Do you think that is enough?
I already know you are out there
La inocente
Pretending to care about our kids
Yet sell them to the highest bidder
Pretending to care about my family
Me!
La inocente
Sleep alone
Wake up to destroy me
Alarm sounds at 5am
And I'm sore
I knocked on your door
Because I loved
Too many
Too often
It's easy for you to talk me into it
But that's my job
Actually,
I'm unemployed
And make six and change every two
But I love
Dare me to pay attention
La inocente
Forgot to keep in touch
Yet wants me
To punch her number
Wants to turn me out

La inocente
I bleed that red and blue
Dye and ink you waste
When you mail me those lies
If only you were original
And who writes that filth
And who is behind
all those *mordidas*?
$50 dollars to tattoo my house
With your brand
Would you take her money?
And how about your other *compas*
Amigos in office?
Come out every other year for you
But sit on their asses
While my cousins get shot
And that girl that got v'ed
In last night
They left her in the middle of the street
Next to your plastic propaganda
And the Vietnam vet tells me
"Welcome to terror town"
I'm scared, but not of you
La inocente.

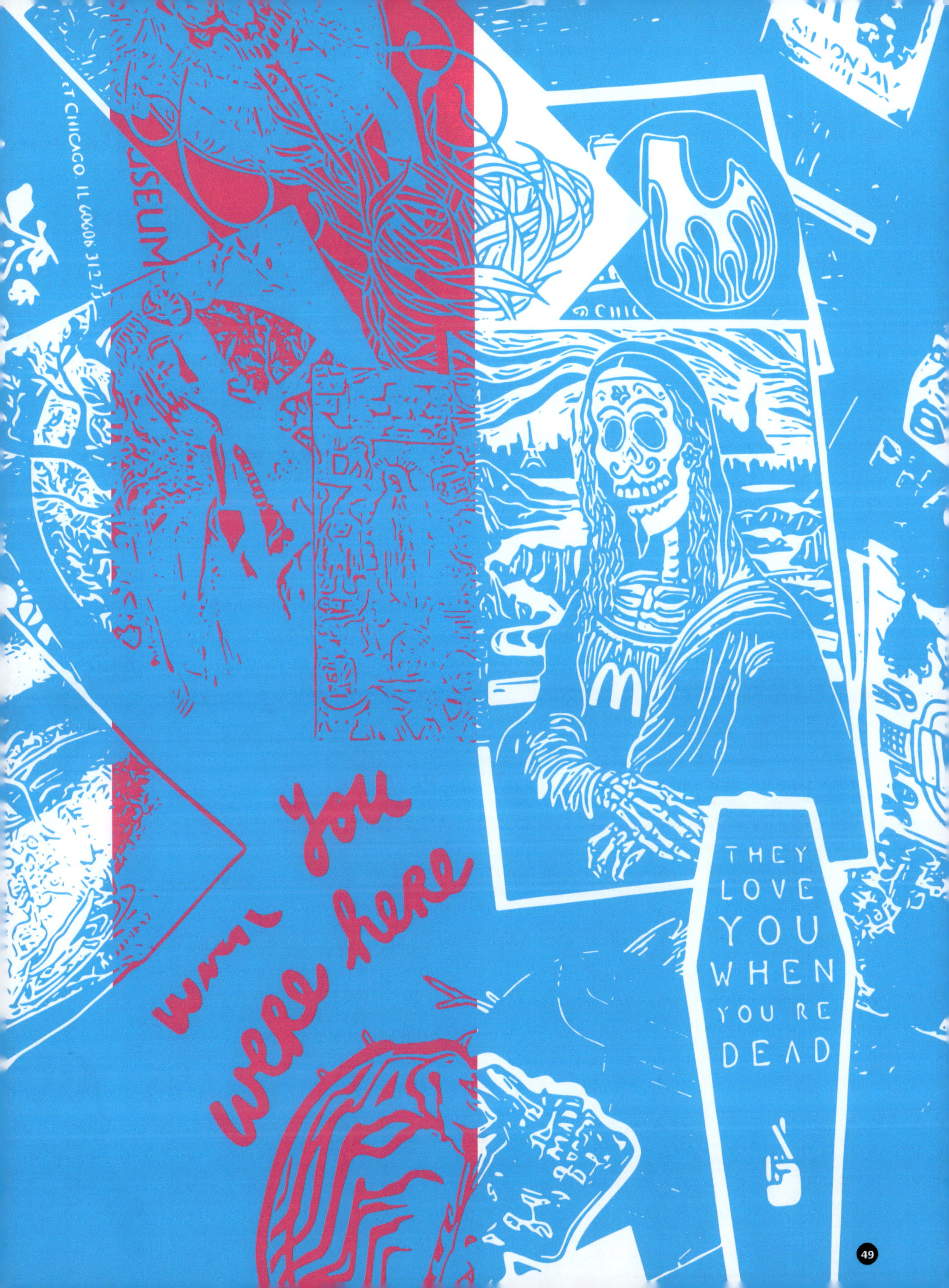
MUSEUM
CHICAGO, IL 60606 3127?
CHIC
you
were here
THEY
LOVE
YOU
WHEN
YOU'RE
DEAD

ELECTRA

White fire
Arriving unannounced
Violent vision
Listen to me strike
Beautiful bolt of Zeus
I dream of you
Like Sophocles and Euripides
Hija de Agamenón
Princesa de Argos
Language was created
and words crawled
limped dragged
To tell your story
Philosophers gave birth to poets
Who traveled to tell of tragedy
But let's rewrite them *mañana*
I dream with you
Your smile
That first time
Saying hello like long lost lovers
Your lips lingered
So I dream
Of your skin
Saludándome
Mezcla perfecta
Spanish Taíno mestiza
You dance with Gypsies
And I try not to be robbed
Of dreams
So I just stare y *me dejas*
I plagiarized those eyes
just to carry them with me

Immortalized on this sheet
I will hold onto
Dreams scream because
morning becomes Electra
When I step inside
Diseased by fantasy
I live on an Isla not *encantadora*
But I still like visitors
in dreams
Your hair is wavy
even when straight and attacks
Waves crashing on chest.
Destroying sand
I'm powerless and honest about it
I try to wake up
but you are passionate
And lust for vengeance.
Kunoichi (ninja assassin)
You tell me your lips are deadly
But then you wear hot pink
And kiss me anyway.
Death by sai.
I'm sorry for Tuesday
But today is Wednesday
And Thursday
I dream with Electra.

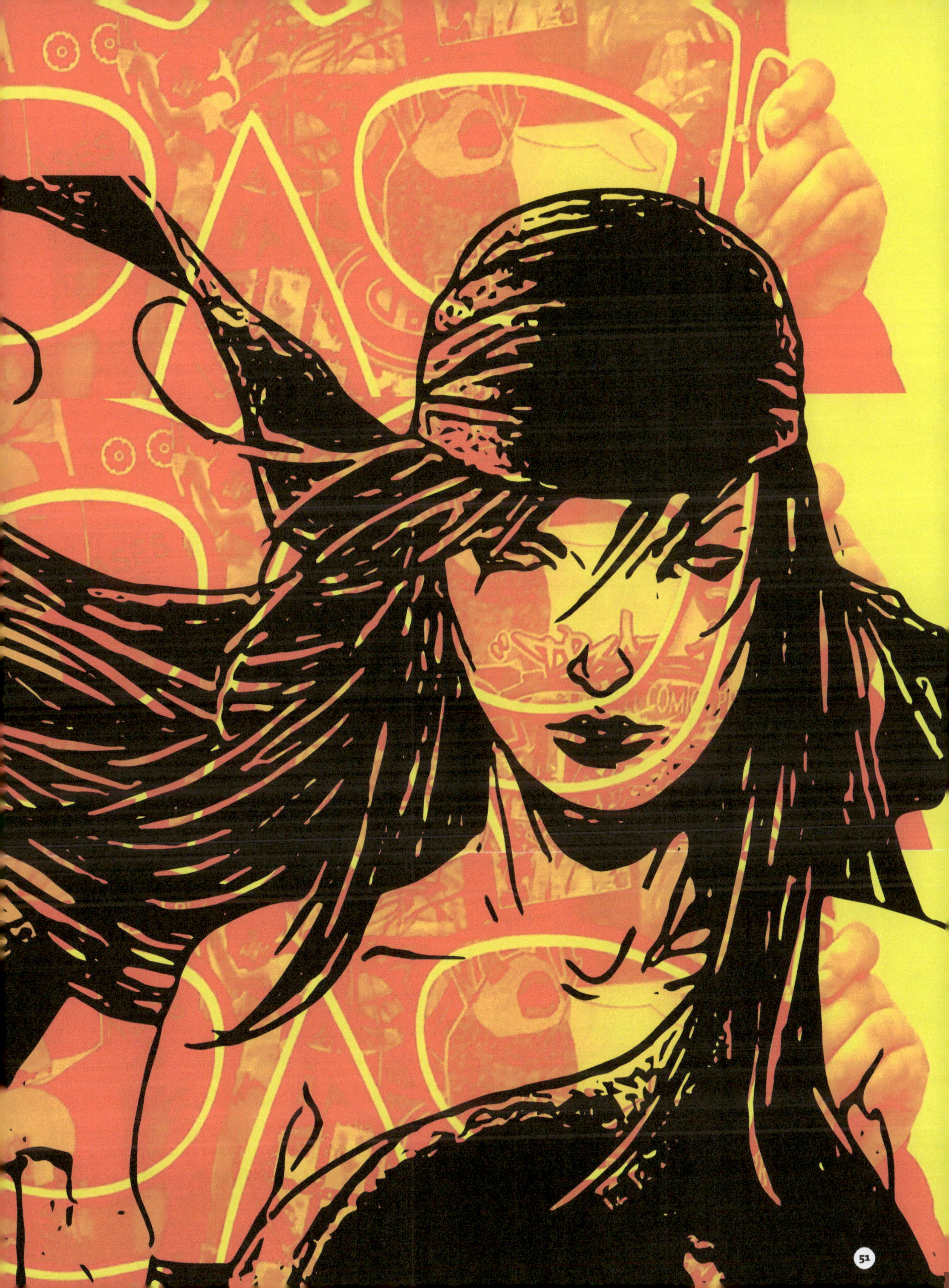

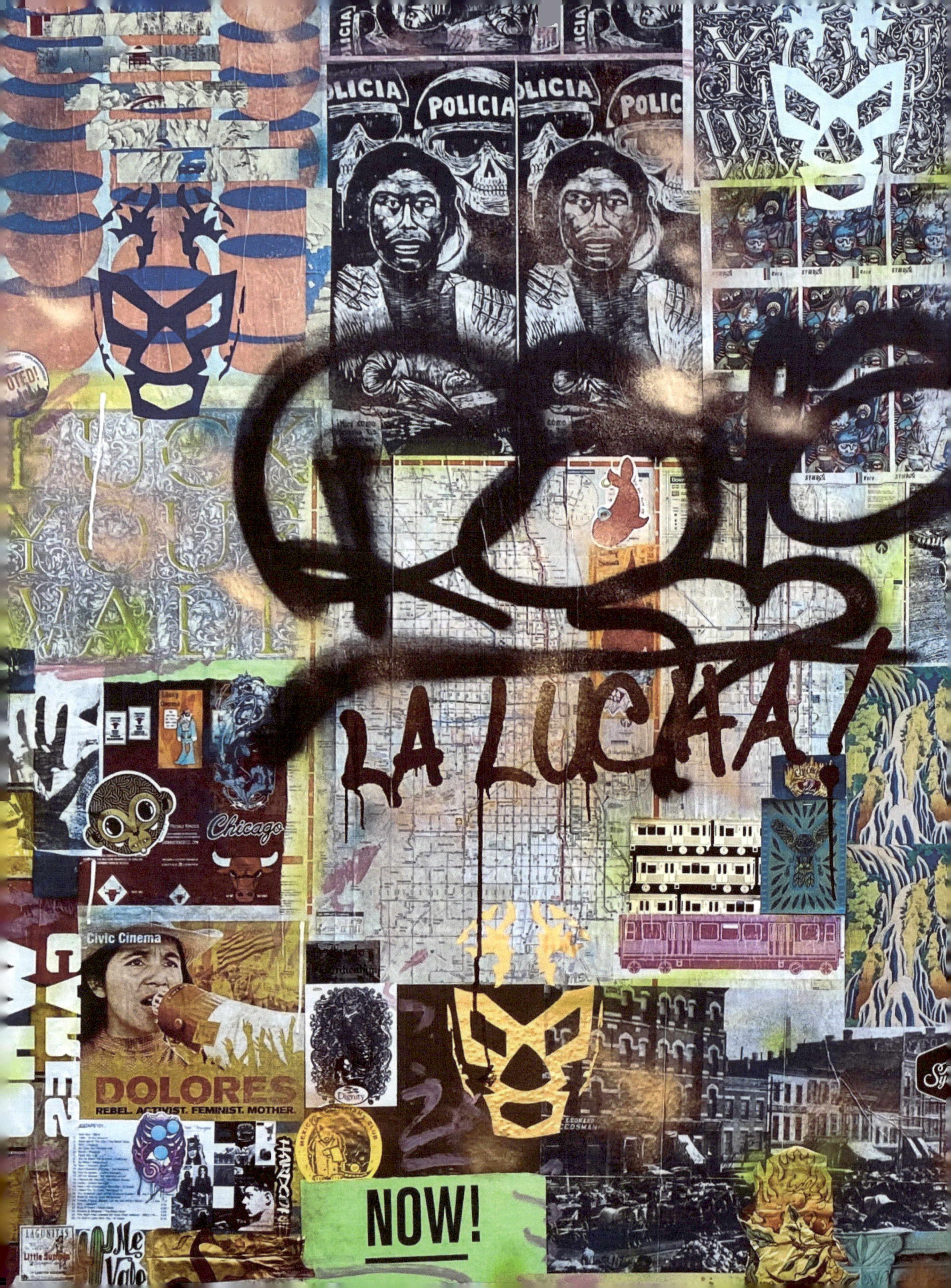

POLICIA
POLICIA
POLICIA
POLIC
LA LUCHA!
Chicago
Civic Cinema
DOLORES
REBEL. ACTIVIST. FEMINIST. MOTHER.
Dignity
NOW!
Lagunitas
Little Sumpin
Me Vale

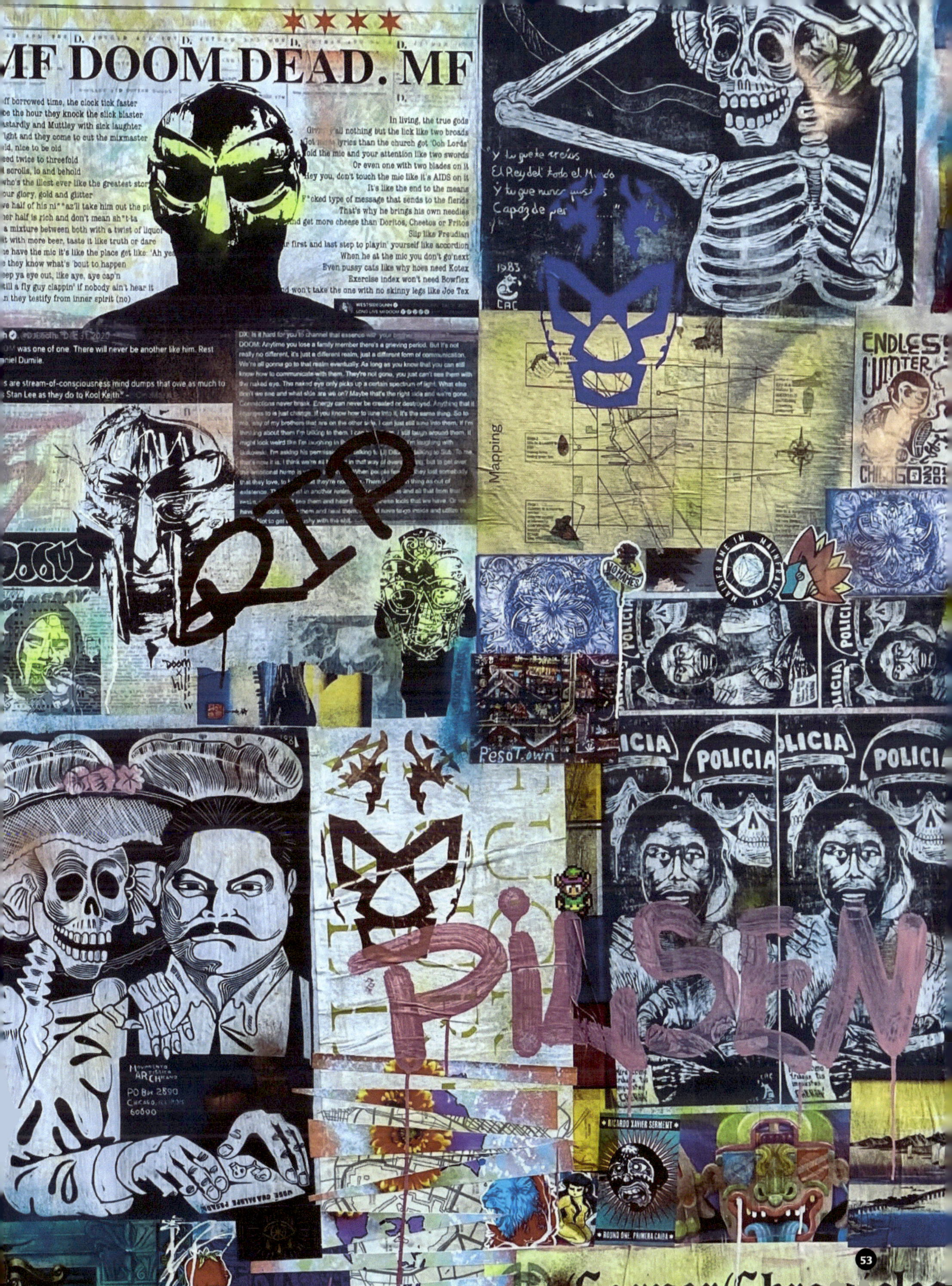
MF DOOM DEAD. MF
PILSEN
POLICIA POLICIA POLICIA POLICI
RIP
ENDLESS WINTER
CHICAGO
Mapping
PesoTown
1983
El Rey del todo el Mundo
Movimiento Artistico Chicano
PO Box 2890
Chicago, IL 60690
RICARDO XAVIER SERMENT
ROUND ONE. PRIMERA CAIDA
WESTSIDE DOOM
LONG LIVE MF DOOM

MAP TRICKS

Chicago starts to
Bleed as these seeds
Disagree with me
Unfriend me. Block me
Dare dynamic and intervene
On my behalf
Strip fast fly straight
Don't push likes for
Simple satisfaction
Don't destroy
just to finish me off
Fresh like ripe *aguacates*
You could not wait to eat
As we sit on park benches
 and bus stops
Dreaming of old times
Old pleasures and old values
Corruption creeps
Veined marble too white to notice
Your caramel mouth
Distant breath
That allows for friends to surprise
And intervene
Be seen, be free
Like belly buttons in July
Although August presents
And September looms
Large like your spectacle
Aura that makes colors fashionable
And things possible
Tracks are removed because they impede
Progress as you undress and tease
Freeze my heart every winter
Just long enough to insert yourself
And remind me of dawn
And of waves that fold away
Into themselves
Thawing what remains of my
Innocence
I return from the viaduct a puddle
Of what remained.

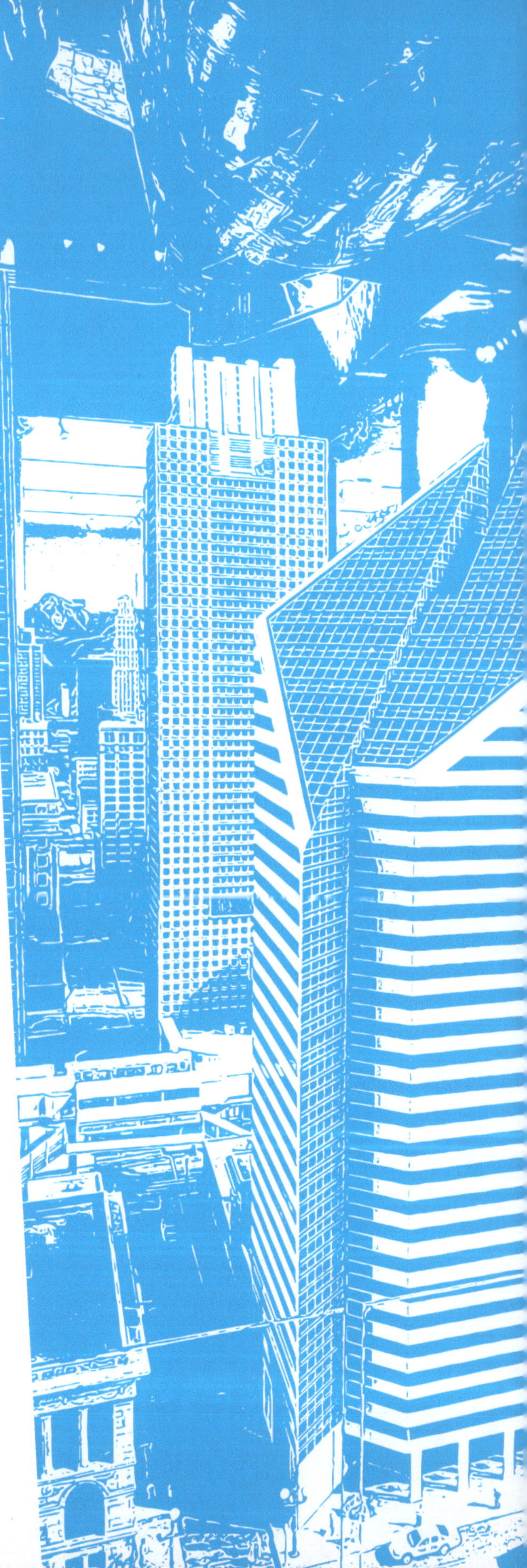

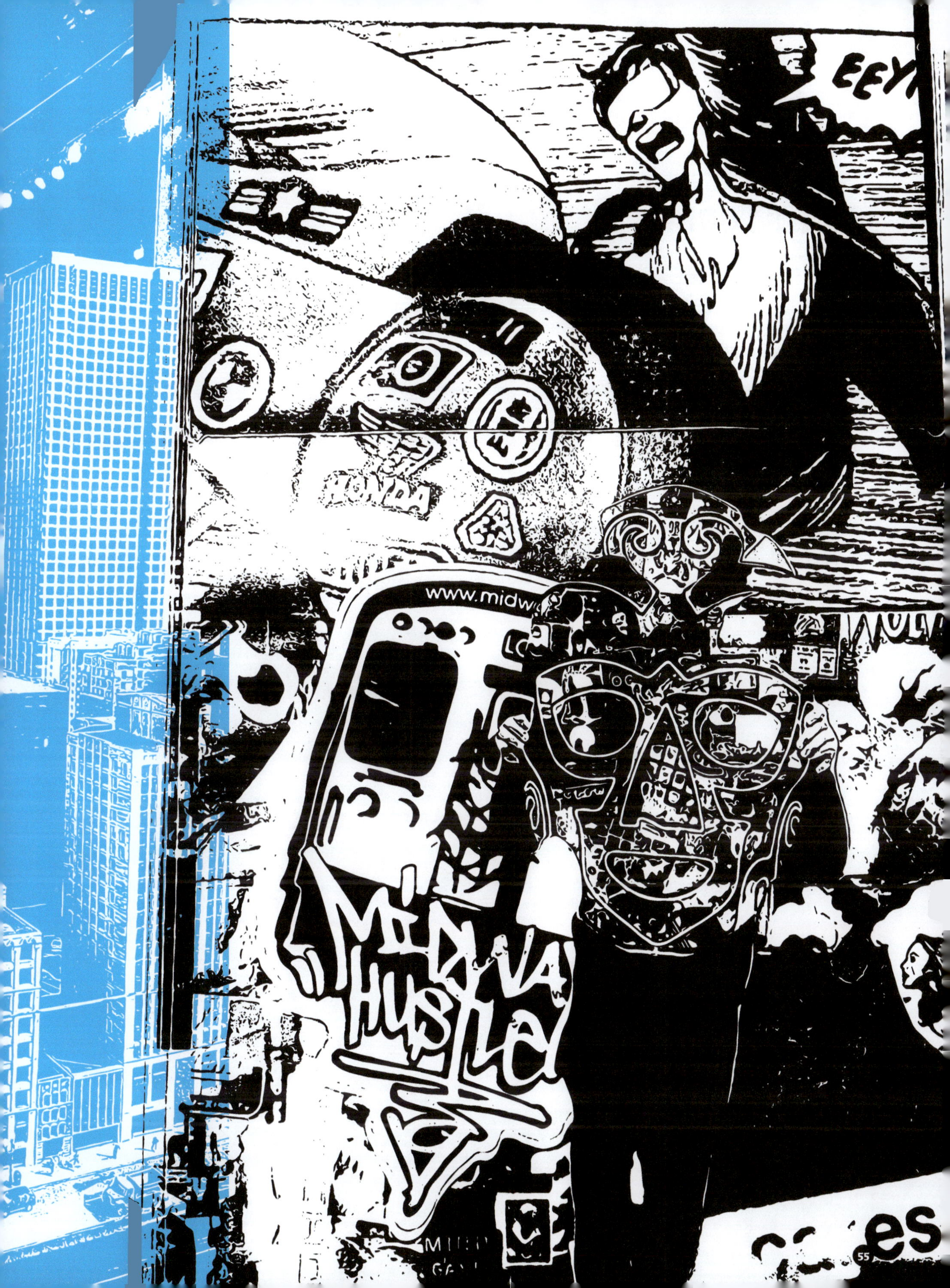
EEY
HONDA
www.midw
MIDWAY
HUSTLE
es
55

4 STARS

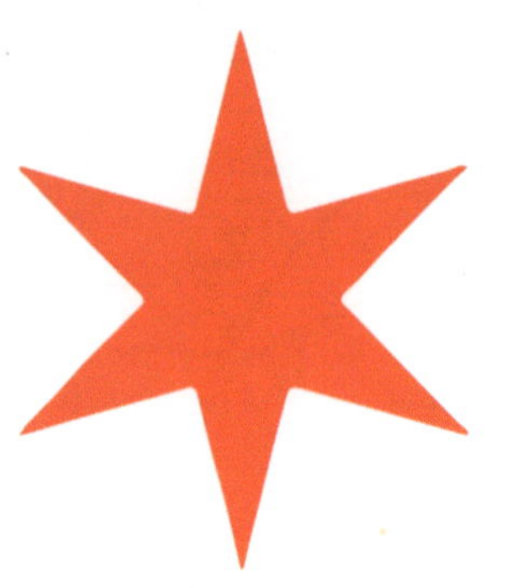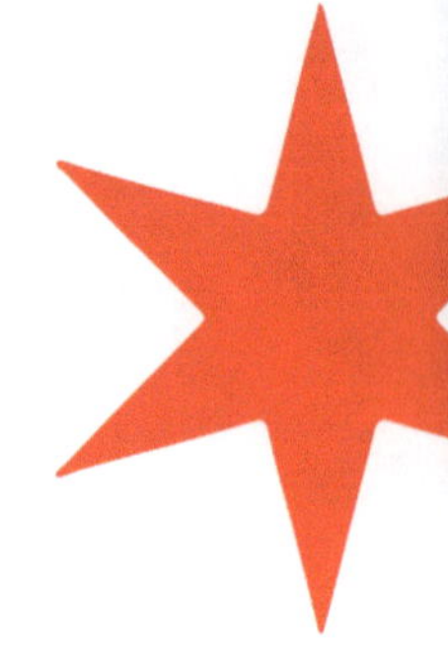

Don't turn around
Lie there dormant
Ixtaccihuatl
White woman
Sleep Chicago
Before I wake you
I mean, Chicago is a woman right?
Second City?
Is light blue really manly?
Onion?
What does that make you think of
Your perfect...and worth the wait
Pero despierta
Wake the fuck up
I am ready to occupy
You mean everything to me
I want to make you cry
Chicago like elevated tracks
I only hold back
To hold your back
Big shoulders
Only because I pull them down
And because Sandburg said so
I am ready to occupy
Black rain
Because your color changes
But never your hair
Gets tugged gently
Till that bottom lip quivers
Bite and occupy
Tongue to tongue to tongue
Your red star
Would not be enough
Because you have four
Chicago, You smell better now
Because you are dirty

A machine that's cranky, oily, windy
But still needs to run
So I occupy you
Like Grant I occupy
Every night my tent gets arrested
Every day I make bail
Chicago listen
To that river.
Those light blue bars through my flag
I especially like that bottom bar
Southern branch, your canal
I occupy, like Panama
I occupy like Washington
did the Delaware I occupy
Like Tribe did Hip Hop I occupy
Like AMLO and pueblo did
Zocalo I occupy. Like Tiananmen
I occupy, Like G8 I occupy
Like every city should
I occupy, Chicago
And so should you.

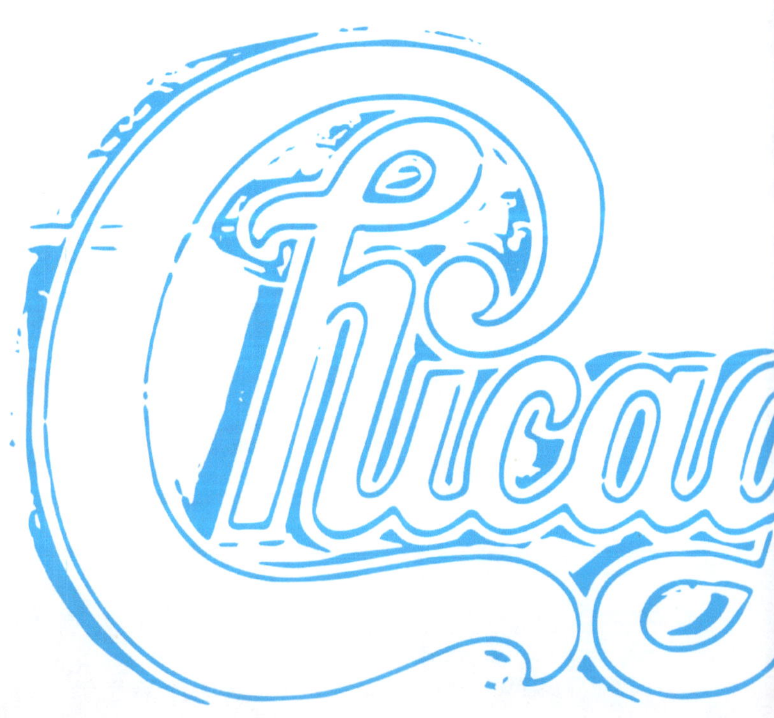

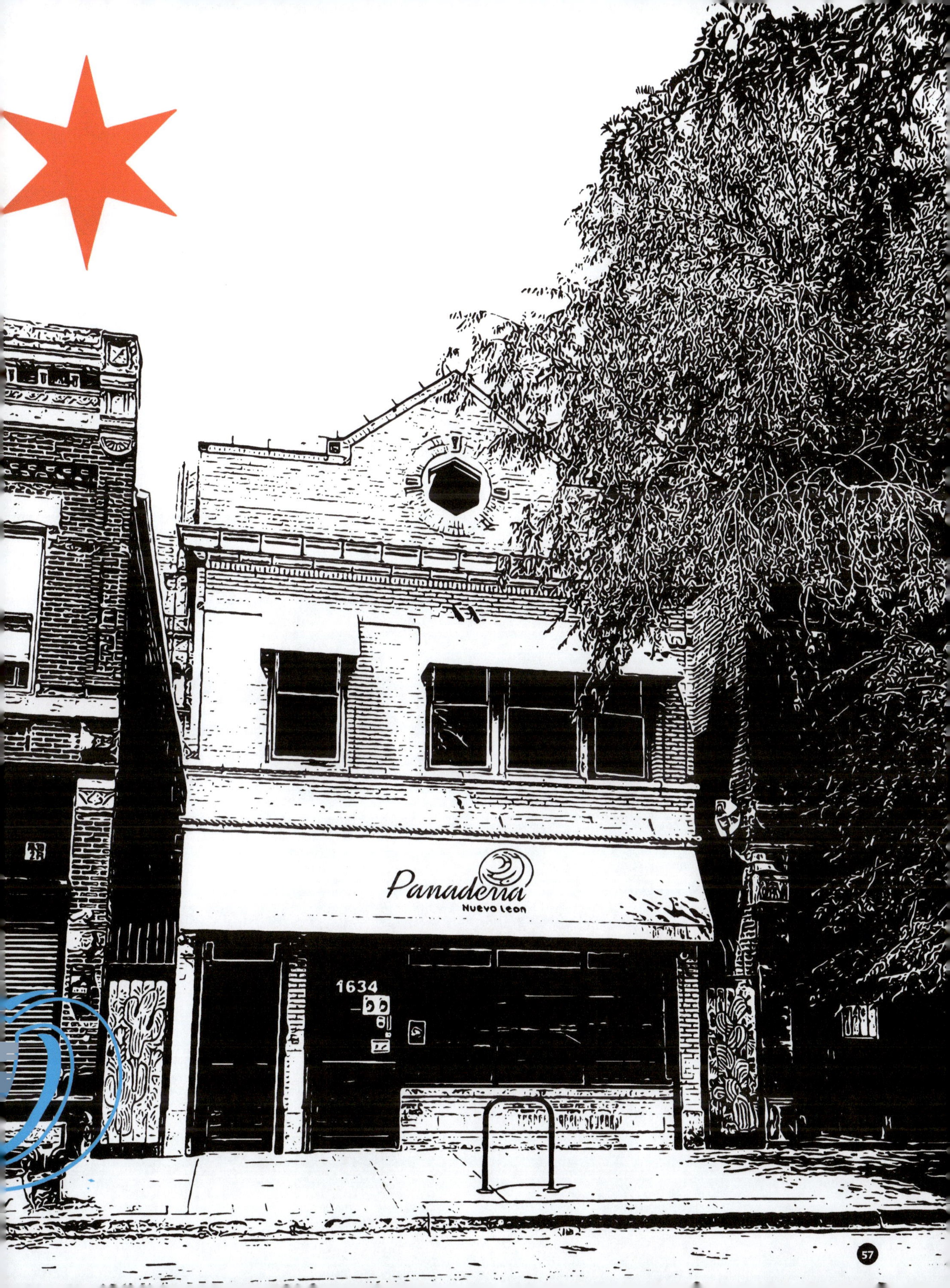

Panaderia
Nuevo Leon
1634

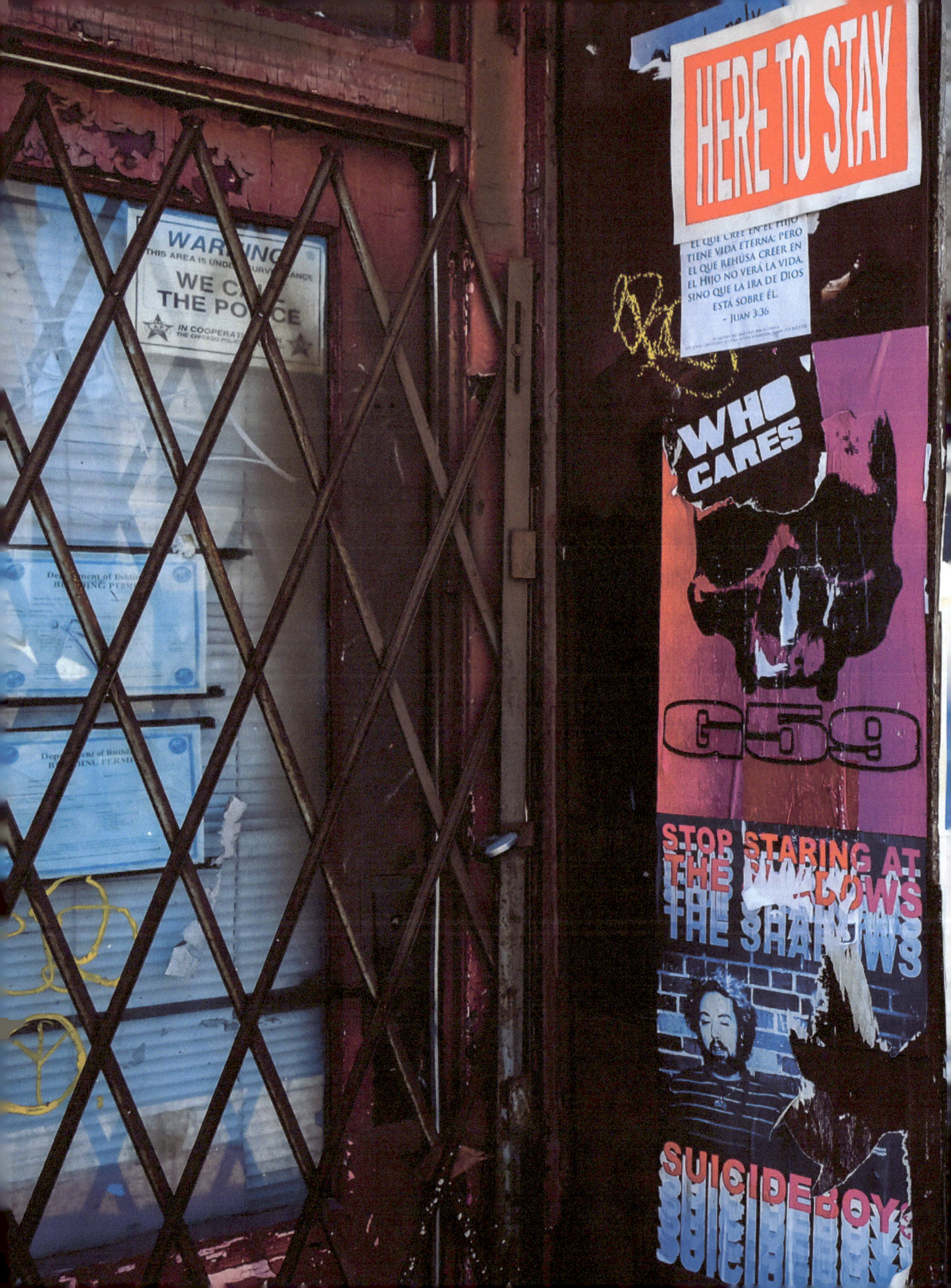

HERE TO STAY
WARNING
THIS AREA IS UNDER SURVEILLANCE
WE CALL
THE POLICE
IN COOPERATION
THE CHICAGO POLICE
Department of Buildings
BUILDING PERMIT
Department of Buildings
BUILDING PERMIT
EL QUE CREE EN EL HIJO
TIENE VIDA ETERNA; PERO
EL QUE REHÚSA CREER EN
EL HIJO NO VERÁ LA VIDA,
SINO QUE LA IRA DE DIOS
ESTÁ SOBRE ÉL.
- JUAN 3:36
WHO CARES
G59
STOP STARING AT
THE SHADOWS
THE SHADOWS
SUICIDEBOY

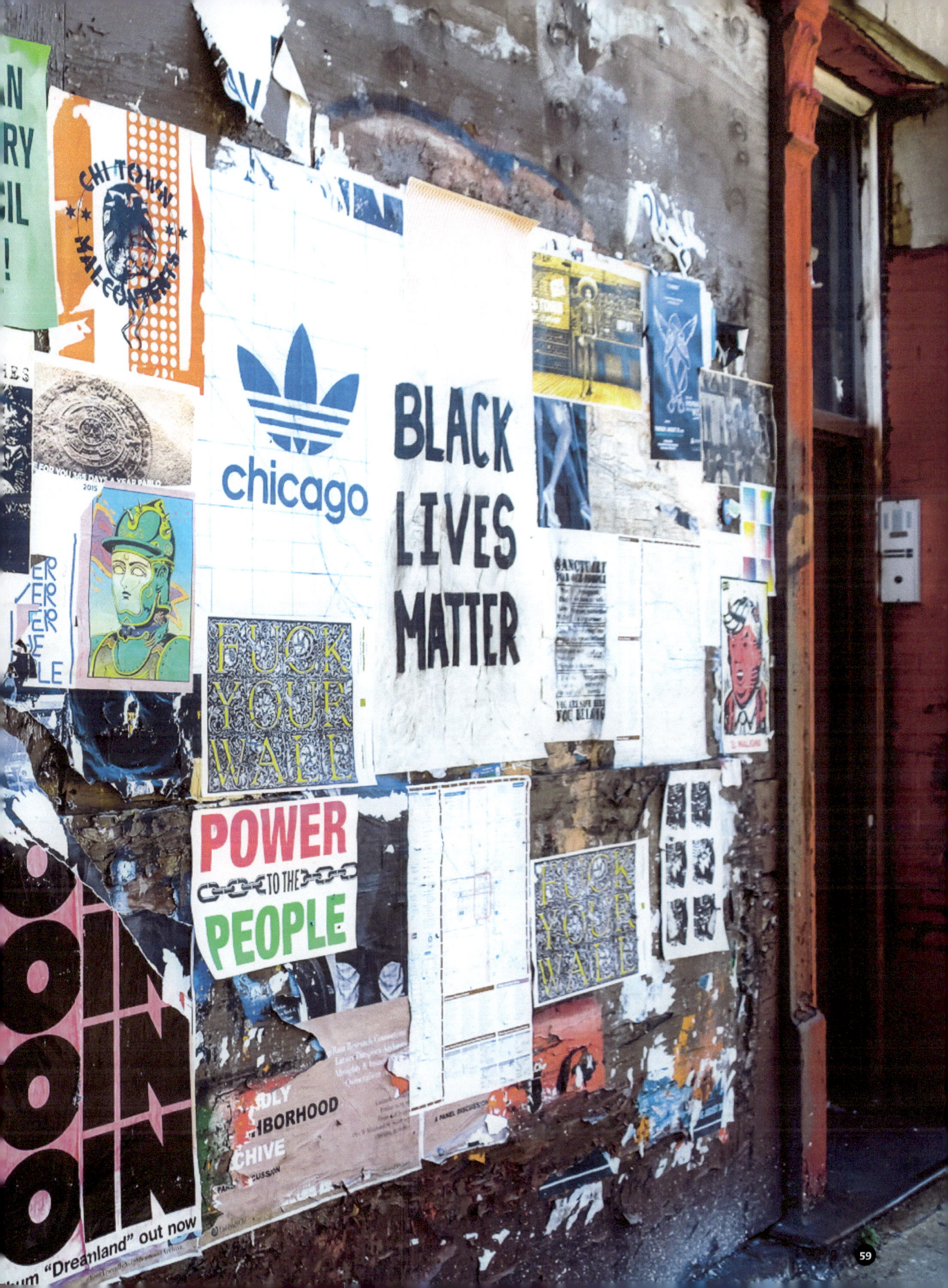
CHI TOWN
MALCONTENTS
chicago
BLACK
LIVES
MATTER
FUCK YOUR WALL
POWER
TO THE
PEOPLE
FUCK YOUR WALL
FOR YOU 365 DAYS A YEAR PABLO
2015
"Dreamland" out now

DIBS STREET

Puros pervertidos
Playing with pelotas
In Pilsen
I have gold copper
chicana con tanta curva
Sizzling *Tejas serpiente*
Esa Ruka bien fina
Y lo sabe
Por eso tiene hata's on Ada
and is down to Dusek my Allport-ante
On the regular
And gets *más asquerosa* on Ashland
Than *las otras*. Yeah
My baby lives on Dibs St.
And she's dirty like my streets
OK so maybe
she leaves my balls
bien Blue Island
A veces but mostly
I Cullerton her Canal or maybe
Carpenter it
I Coulter her by the *greñas*
And give her my Cermak
Si...
My baby lives on Dibs St.
And she's dirty like my streets
Diabólica Damen danzando toda la noche
Me Leavitt *todo desbaratado*
Leaves my loin draggin' on Hoyne
And my *lengua bien* Halsted
15,16,17 Laflin all the way
Con sonrisa de diamantes
Fangs only for Loo-*mis ojos* here.
Yeah
My baby lives on Dibs St.
And she is dirty like my streets
Diez y ocho dientes
Me despiertan

Mordiendo mis Morgan-os
Mis insides
May no longer hold
Coronas from all the holes
Ni Miller
Lights up mi Peoria each time her
Labios me piden Paulina
19,20,21
Le doy más Oakley
23,24,25
I must be doing it right *porque*
Me rasguña my Racine
And starts Throop-ing me even harder
What I tell you!
My baby lives on Dibs St.
and she's dirty like my streets
Pero sabes lo que es lo mejor
Her Sangamon *sabe a limón*
Bien dulce like honey y *Patrón*
My tip finds Union
And 26 slow thrust more Wolcott
My Wood gets Western
Y la veintiséis, y la veintiséis
Everyone knows
she is the *más* filthy
Villita.

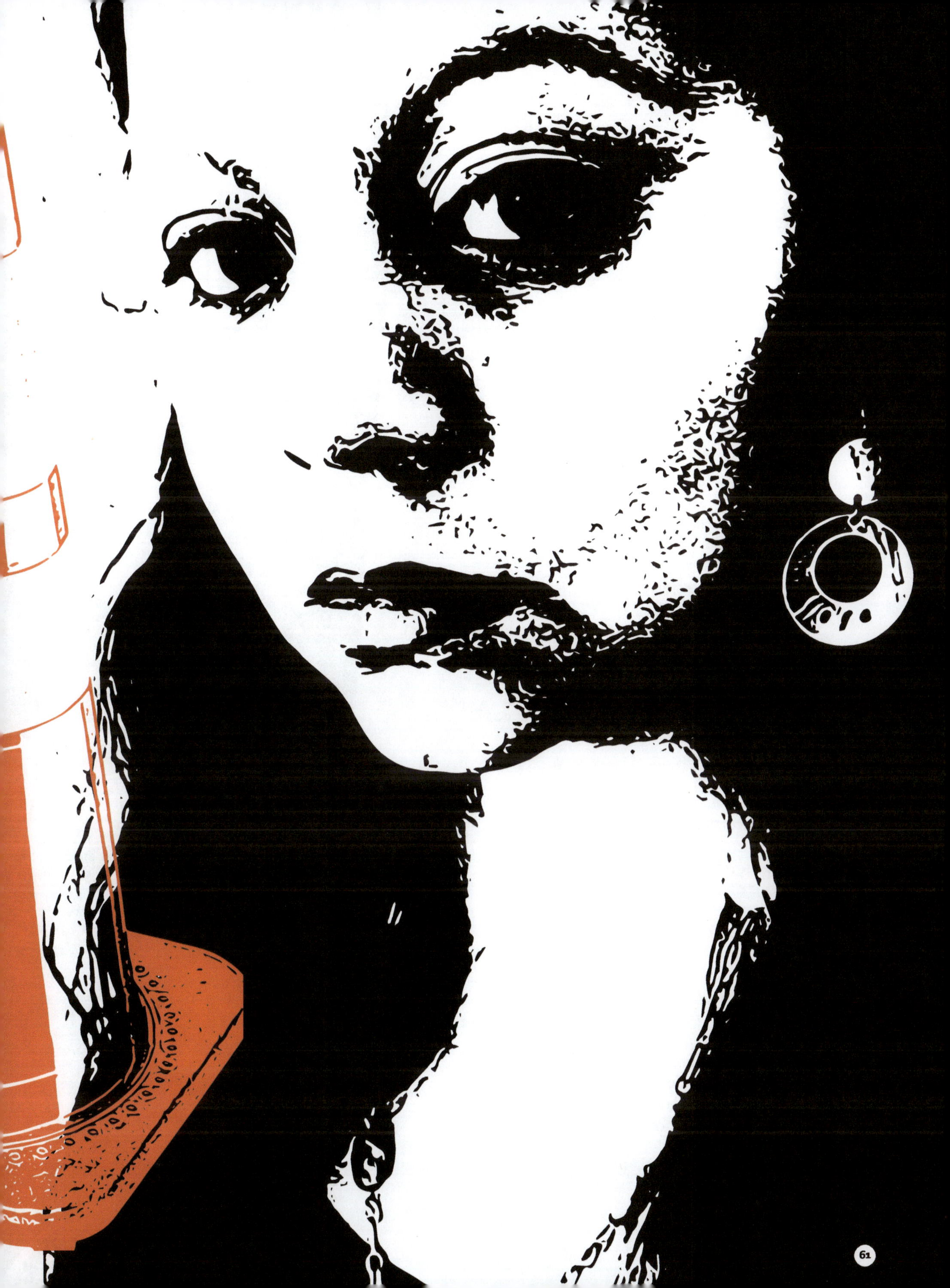

TELL ME

If you are listening
Tell me why my stomach bleeds
without staining my hands?
Tell me I can dive for dreams
without getting wet?
Tell me you no longer need
Cheerios but still need HoneySmacks?
Tell me, tell me, tell me
How the rainbows lost their colors
without ever shutting their eyes?
Why the forest is black with lust
And the night green with greed?
Tell me why strawberries
Are still red like hell's eyes
but still my favorites
Tell me why staring at you never tires
And why your lips are always
drenched by fires?
¿Dime por que los pétalos
nunca han sido tan suaves como tu voz?
¿Dime por que duermes
con dos almohadas
Y yo con una?
¿Dime que lucharas en la revolución
Y pregúntame donde está mi pistola?
Dime, dime, dime
Como tu uña corto mi labio
Y ni me di cuenta
¿Por que te persiguen los ángeles
Y donde escondes el diablo?
¿Dime por que la luna floja
sale a buscarte por la noche?
¿Dime por que el sol trabajador
se levanta cuando abres tus ojos?
¿Dime por que extraño tus labios
si es que realmente no los conozco?
¿Dime por que sigo
esperando que bailes conmigo?
¿Dime mujer, si me estas escuchando?.

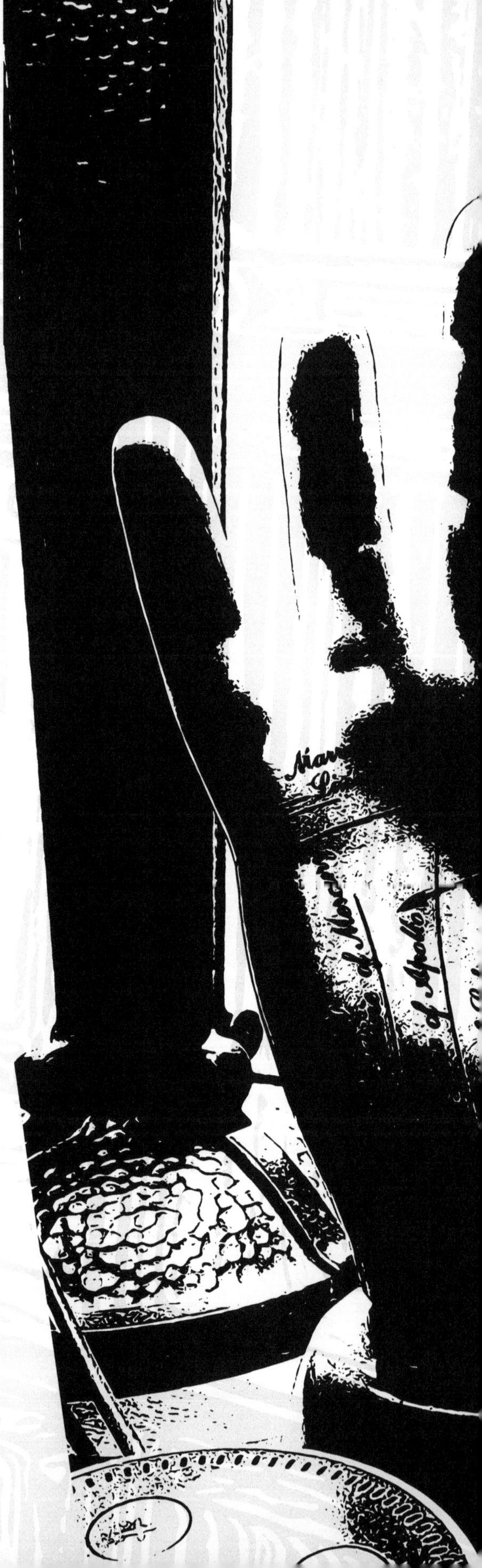

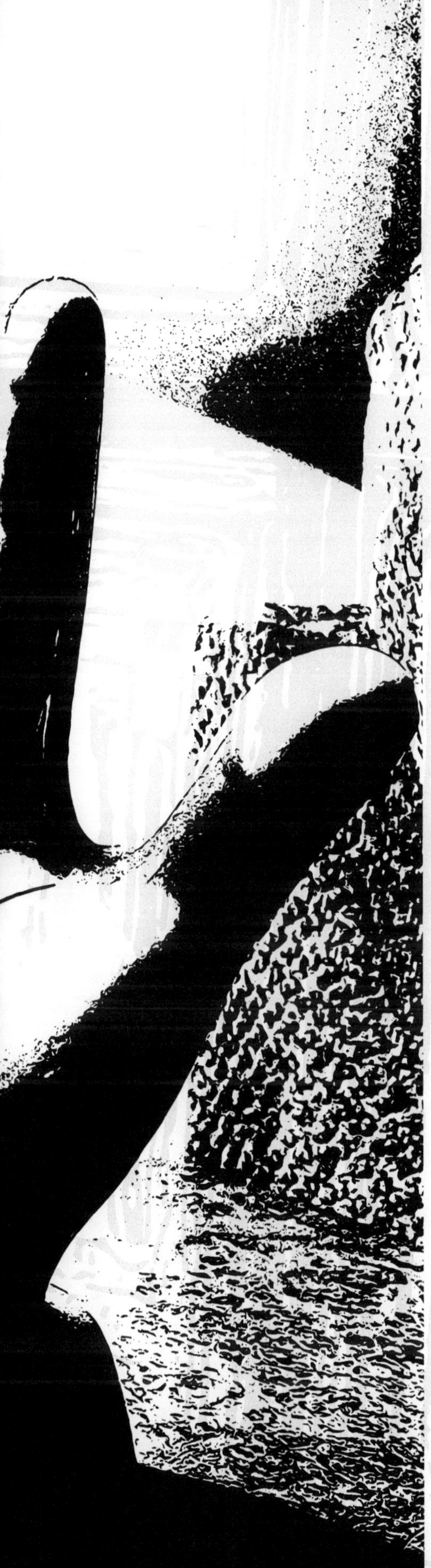

187

One hundred seventy blocks
separate our lies
One hundred sixty three words
till this poem dies with microphone
One hundred fifty two times
I stared at that same spot on your body
One hundred thirty eight times too many
But could I really help it?
I'm sick and those other
Fourteen times mariposas
One hundred seventeen seconds
Pass between truths
And I still know nothing
But who fucking cares
When all we have left are
*Noventa y cuatro palabras bien
pronunciadas*
Only because you can't
I can and do
Eighty one strangers
Thought it would not last
And you told me it didn't matter
Sixty six was a route that was wandered
And only off by a few digits
Fifty one times I woke up last night
Scared to let go of past number
Thirty six trips our lips said hello
Twenty nine times they said goodbye and
Twenty two acquaintances
They thought they could share
Fourteen flowers
Twelve timely tantrums
Nine innings
Seven days
Five fingers
Three poems
One.

TODAY

My words will not be enough
Today
God will be cursed out
Today
We will watch Cubs baseball
Today
We will wish the Bears were better
Today Little Village cries
And Pilsen is jealous
Today *paletas*
And *elotes* are half off
Today grown men will cry
Today we will dig up old comics
And read them to our kids
Today we will all be Jedi
Today we will wheat paste
Today we will be Hoodsy
Today we will paint
Today we will watch all the good
Star Wars Movies
Today we will buy collector toys
Today we shop for gadgets
Today I get to go to my rooftop
and scream
Rat Tat Tat tat tat
Today I get to be myself
Today I get to be witty
Today I get to be a teacher
Today I get to love my neighbor
Today I own 26th St.
Today I am Villarte y Villapalooza
Today I screen print
Today I will make shirts
TodayI get to dress up for Halloween early
Today I design logos and posters
Today
Chicago has 5 stars
Today
I carve a woodblock
Rat Tat Tat tat tat tat
Today our streets have colors

Today you left us an angel
Today your organization
 lost its first letter
Today symbols mean nothing
Today actions mean everything
Today blasters and sabers
get handed out
Rat Tat Tat Tat
Today
We go to war
Today the commissioner lost
Today our neighborhood
is up for grabs
Today
You inspire and give back
Today
Our name is Carlitos
Today
These words will not be enough
Today
We will hug each other
Today
Rat Tat Tat
I will share Columbia
stories of you
Today
I will be honest
Today
I will light up a room
Today
You teach us about Grace
Today
I will give everything
Today
You became a hologram
Today
I will start to run
So that I can catch up to you.

For Elias "Tat" Corral

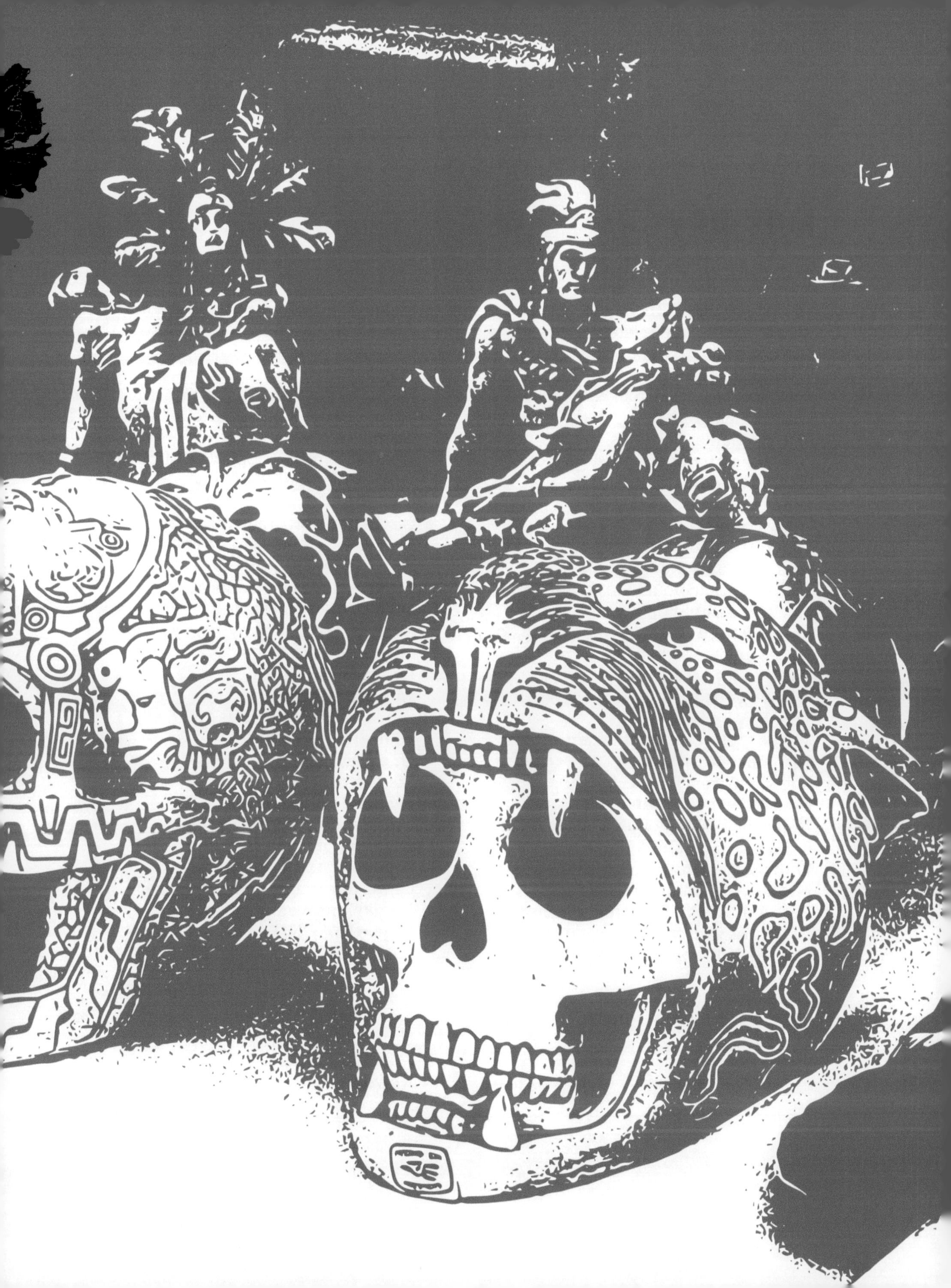

MAY DAY

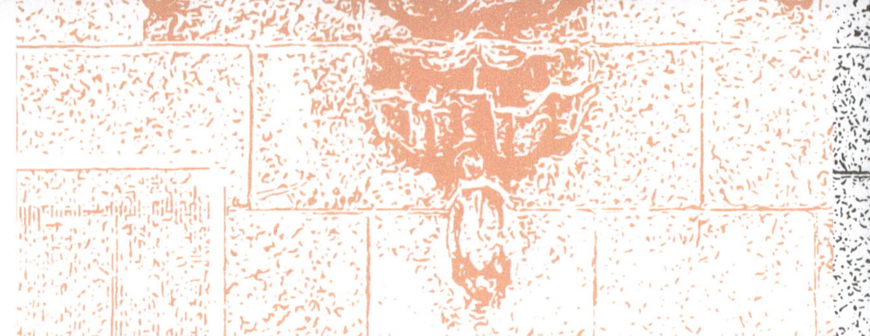

Fell in bed April 30th
With more filthy four letter words
Floating about than normal
Woke up May 2nd
Sore, late, beat, cold, fuck
I missed May Day
March, chants, demands, unions
Freedoms, charades, masses, colors
Being occupied
I slept through the whole damn thing
I only remember my lips grazing
Your dirty mouth and kissing
Your neck and cheek until
I traced back to your lips
Meeting, melting only for a second
As you floated weightless above my body
Asleep, in dream, in love
But what's your excuse
Why do you ignore
That 1% whore
Maybe that word is a little harsh
For someone in love
But where were you yesterday
Consumed by cunning
Or just working another
8, 9, 10, 12 hour shift
With reluctant lunch
Maybe a 10 minute smoke break
But who pays for those doctors visits
And those overpriced blue, purple, pink
Shaped daily combo candies
Maybe
Maybe the city was putting her
Fat ass belly on your throat
Sick fuck

Meanwhile taking pictures of you
Charging you $100 for the pleasure
Of seeing yourself online
Maybe
Maybe paying mortgages to
Bailout banks kept you occupied
Or maybe
ComEdComcastPeoplesGasTargetATT
VerizonTmobileBPBestBuy
CitgoShellCocaColaPepsiWalmartApple
CiscoMicrosoftAmazonDisney
Kept your interest while they took
Your interest
Another day another dolla
I used to like that saying
But it's not earned anymore just spent
Maybe you spent the day
As a local politician
Talk talk talking
While sell sell selling us out
To the highest bidder
Or closest friend
Kissing babies and shaking
My hand while taking
Hard earned union members dues
Maybe your feet hurt
Or aren't good with crowds
Or maybe you wish those
Mexikkkins weren't taking all our jobs
Maybe Fox, CNN, ESPN
Local news, YouTube and Kardashians
Fried your brain a little too hard
Maybe morning mourning of D. Rose
Early playoff departure kept you away from
Union Park
Mami it's too close to the United Center
No voy

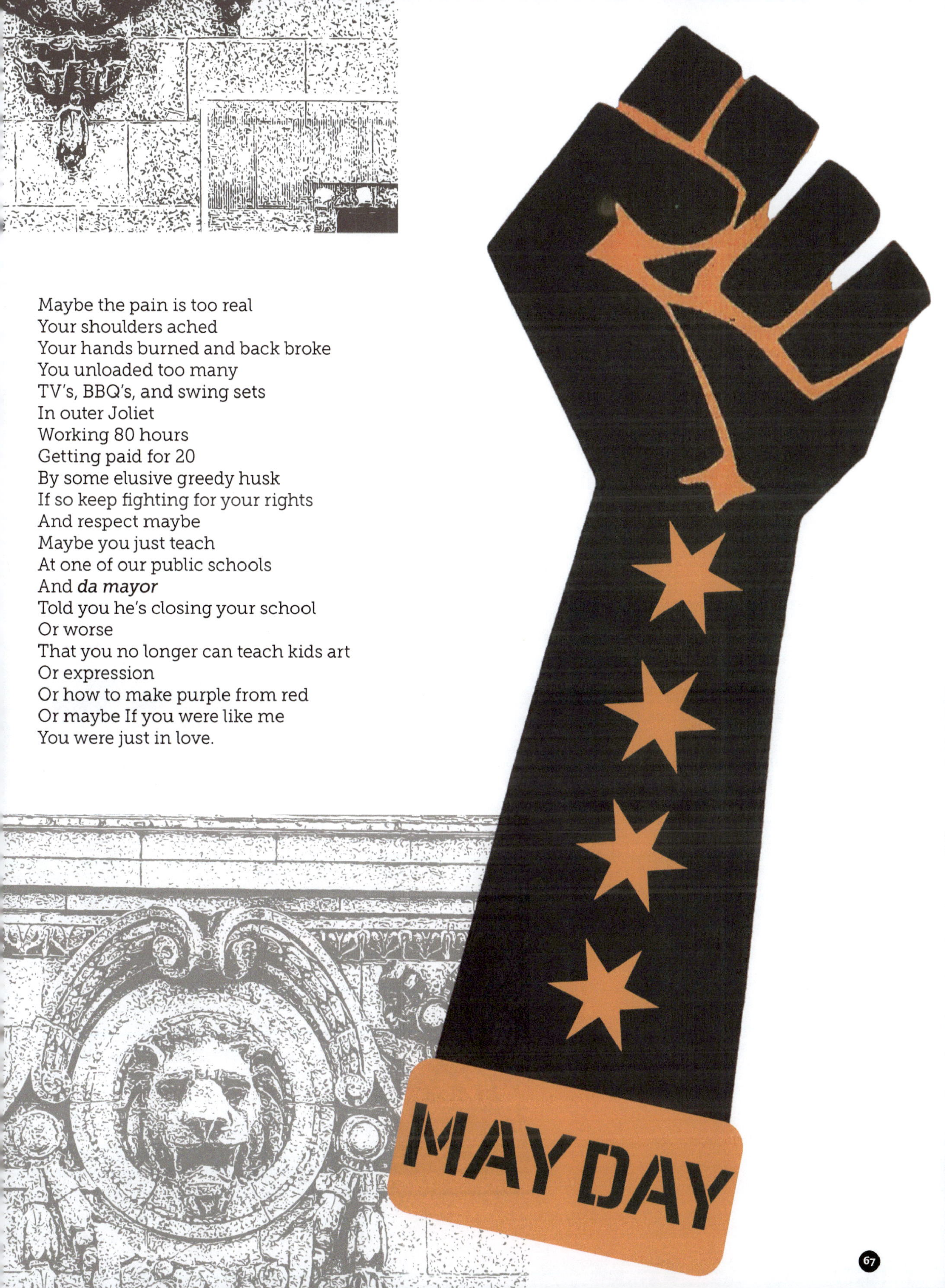

Maybe the pain is too real
Your shoulders ached
Your hands burned and back broke
You unloaded too many
TV's, BBQ's, and swing sets
In outer Joliet
Working 80 hours
Getting paid for 20
By some elusive greedy husk
If so keep fighting for your rights
And respect maybe
Maybe you just teach
At one of our public schools
And *da mayor*
Told you he's closing your school
Or worse
That you no longer can teach kids art
Or expression
Or how to make purple from red
Or maybe If you were like me
You were just in love.

VEINS

l Iove it when you are alive,
I hate it when you deprive
So I just take
Take bits, and pieces
Of you
Besides
That is all you offer
Anyway
Little bites are allowed
Like newborn zombie learning
But I want more
So I take you
Like Eve did that apple
Everywhere, anytime
Day, night
The devils horns twist and squeeze
I spit the seeds out of my mouth
Only to speak with you
Gods whisper heats my cheek
And allows me to keep living
This manic dream
Take five felonies to court
Take friendly fire
Take out those ferocious fangs
And devour me
Tenderly please
Idiotically and without sense
I step onto this stage
And take my time
So that this poem

Lasts
As long as
Your pause
And press play
In your jungle
But let me be your green
Your monster movements and
Tiny moments marinate
And destroy me
Fire ants to my honey
Take my body
Drink from these open veins
Take my eyes and feast
Your body already
left its imprint
Your scent still lingers
And this Tecate
tastes just like you
Salud!

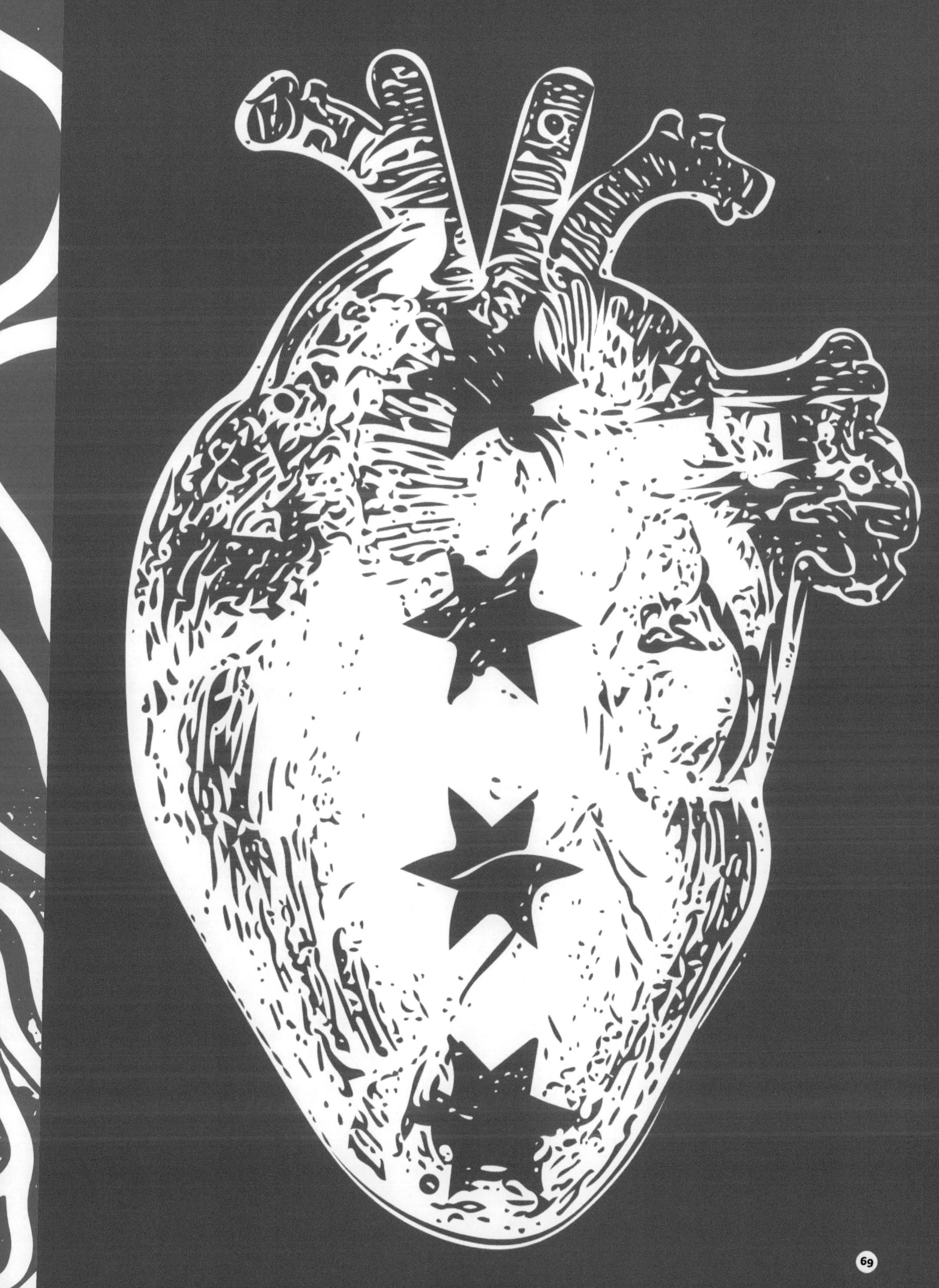

1995

I don't know
what happened last night
But this morning
I awoke next to a woman
Something was different about her
She wasn't the usual beauty
I'm used to waking up to
Don't get me wrong,
she was beautiful
At least her naked
shoulders were as
My eyes followed
Her smooth polished back
Up her neck till they met her hair
Cascades of rich 24k gold
Man, I could not take my eyes
off of them
I wondered what her name was
I was curious
I was ignorant
'Till she turned around
I was drawn into
her pale blue eyes
Then
I knew what had happened
I knew her name
Her name was Colonization
I had been sleeping with the enemy
For five hundred years
She tried to tell me she loved me
But I could still smell
the blood on her breath
I could still feel
the heartbeats of my fallen people
Screaming
The struggle continues!
¡La Lucha Continúa!

 Pocho Love: Pilsen Heart Beats to Chicago Streets

Mural by Camilo Cumpián. @camiloc2c

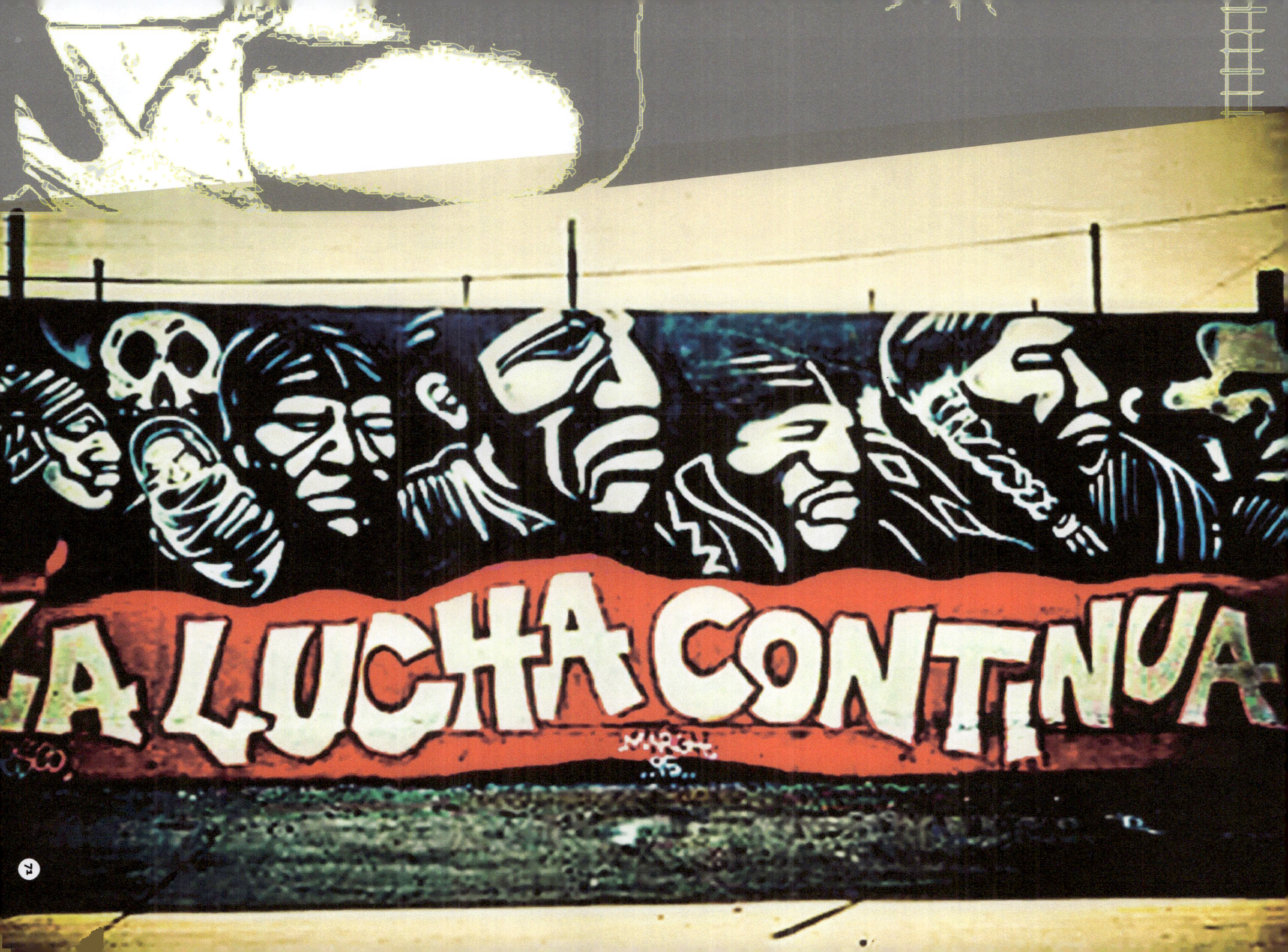
A LUCHA CONTINUA

Corner Chronicles

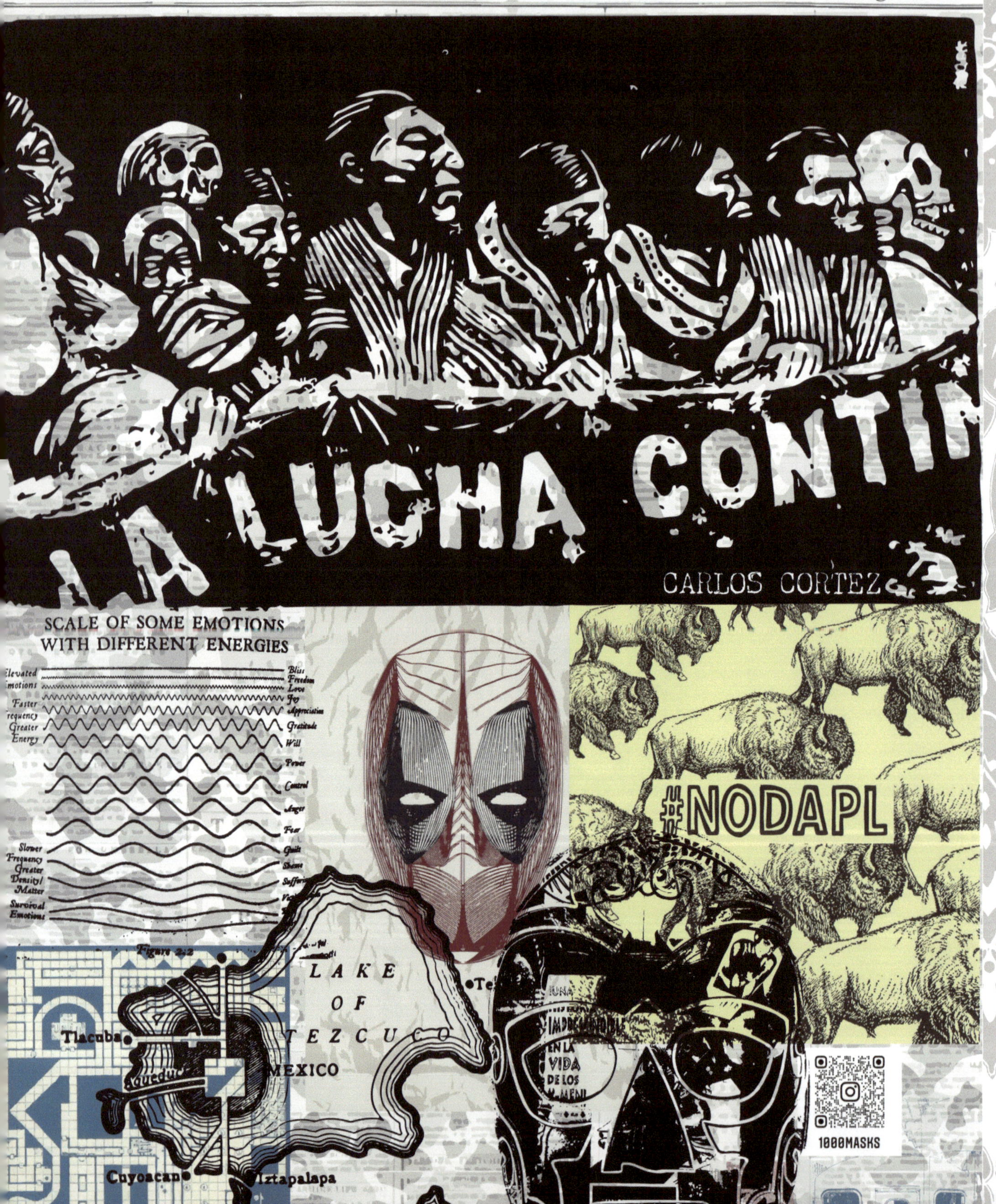

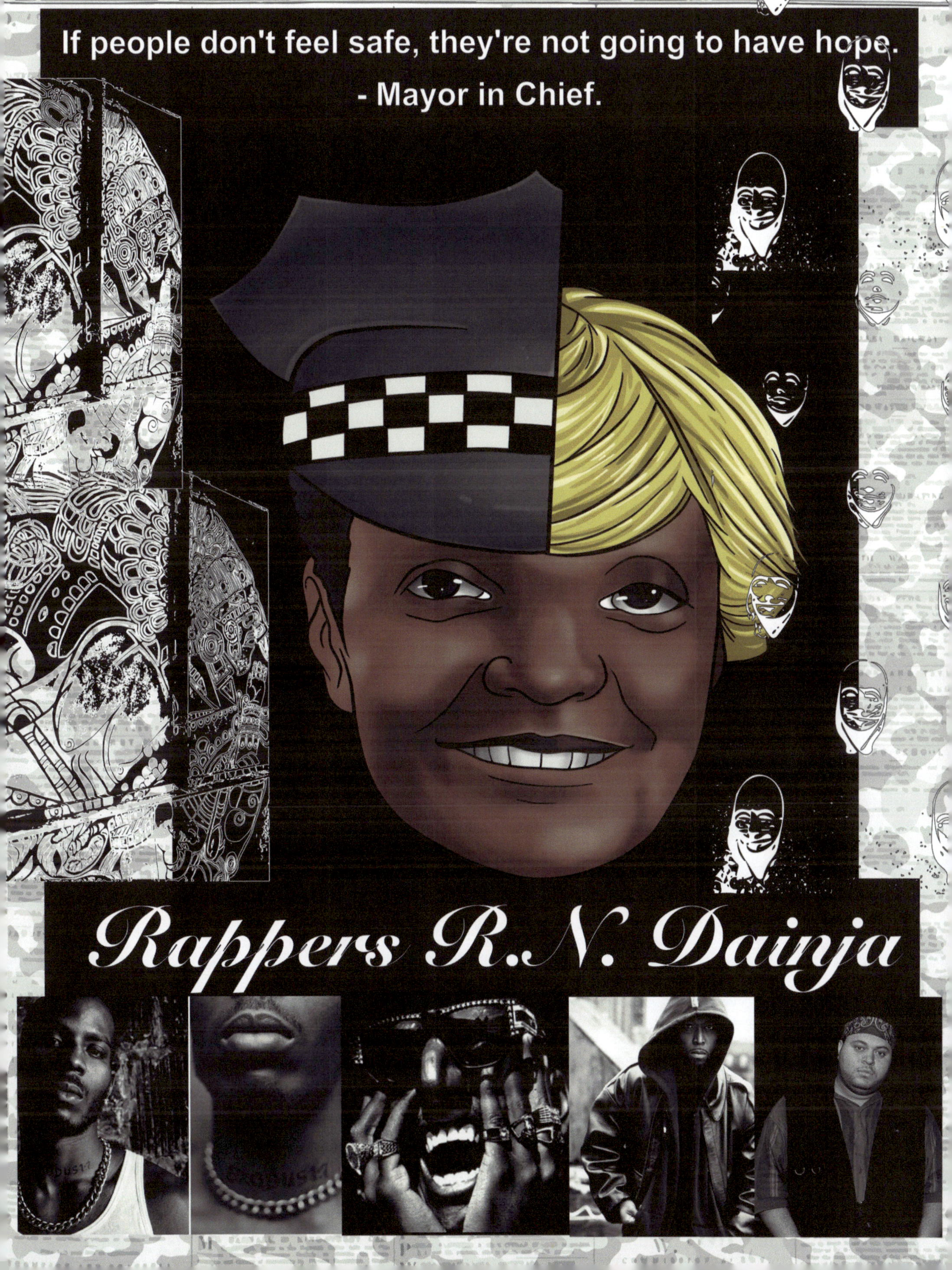

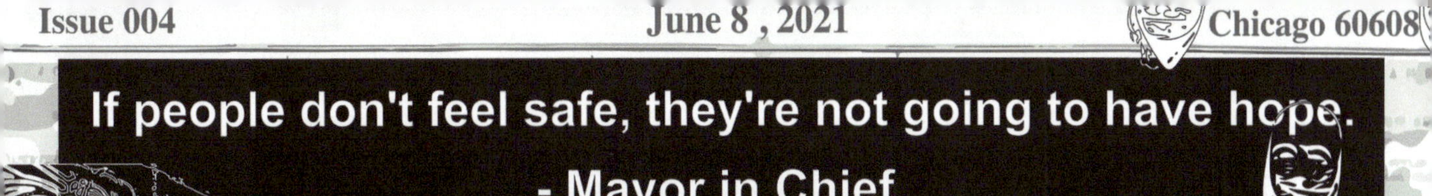

Rappers R.N. Dainja

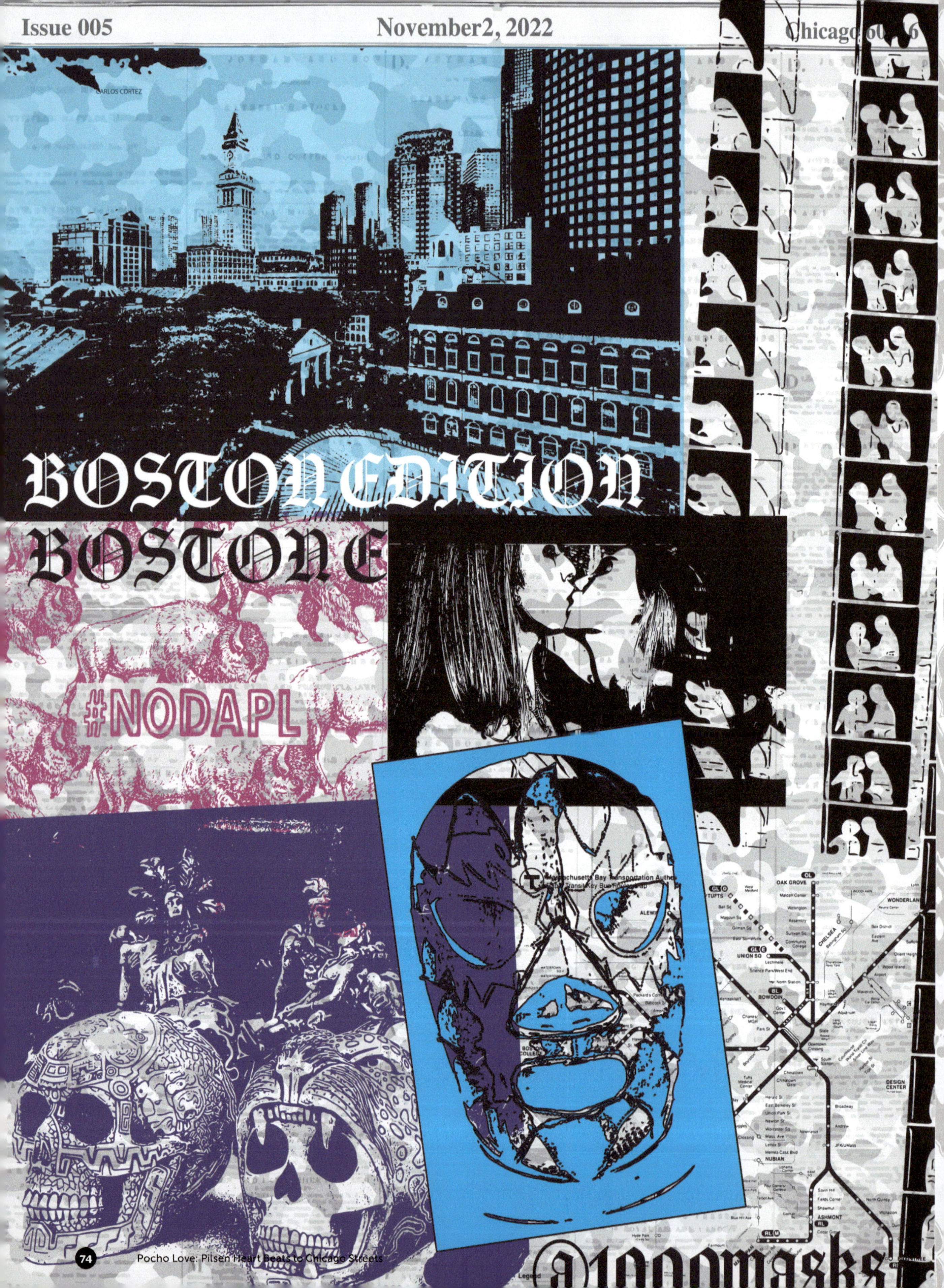

Pocho Love: Pilsen Heart Beats to Chicago Streets

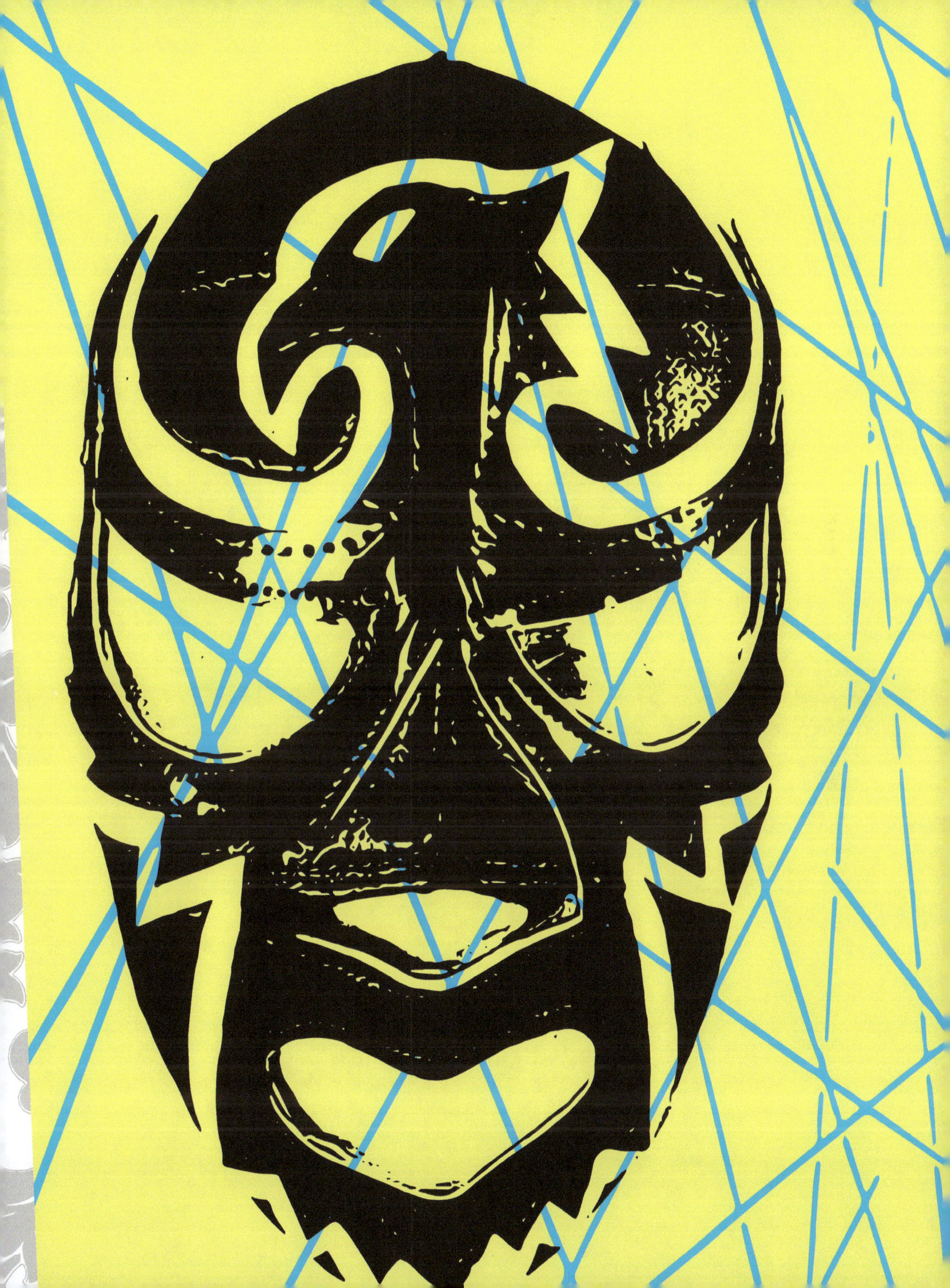

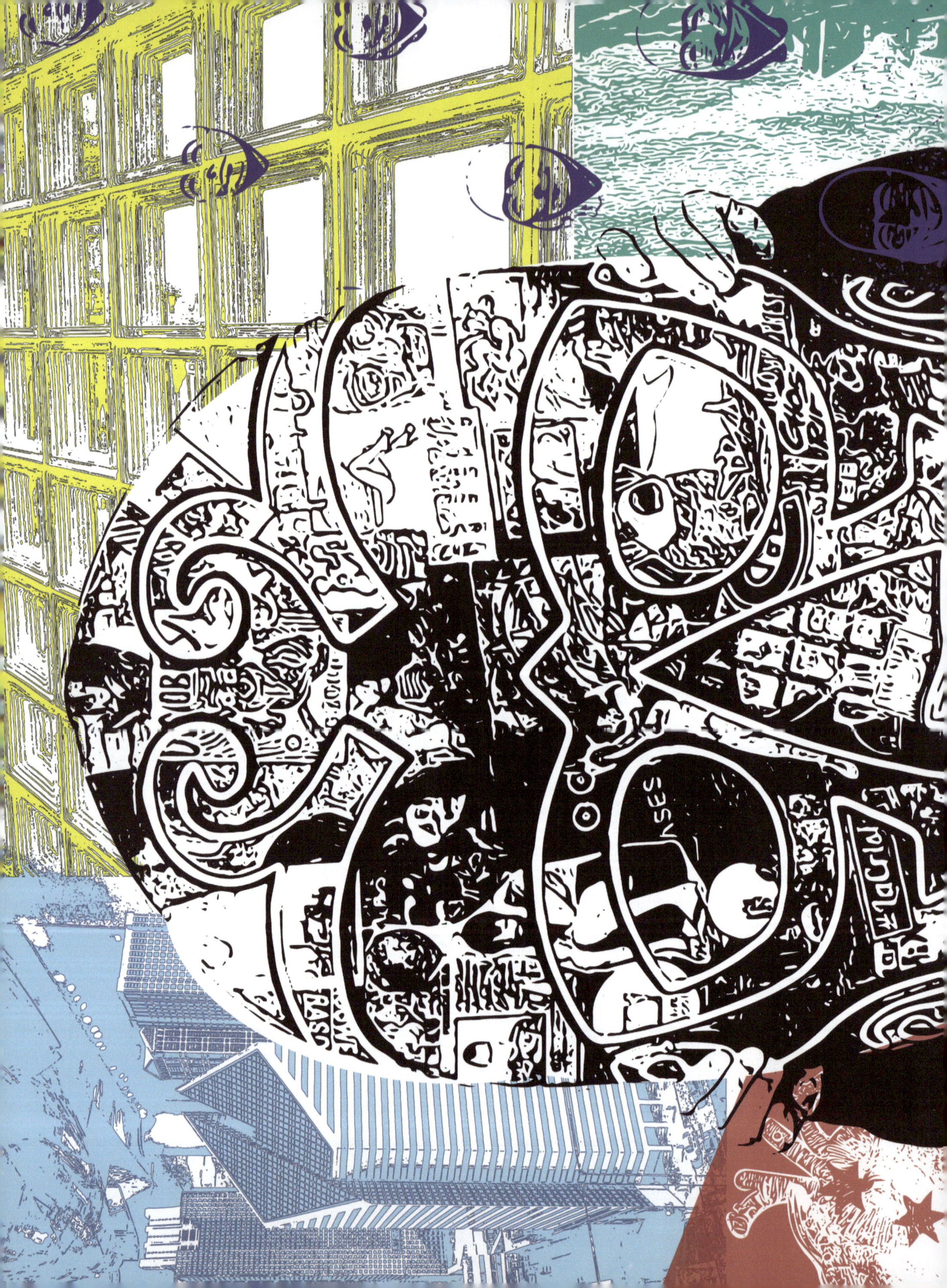

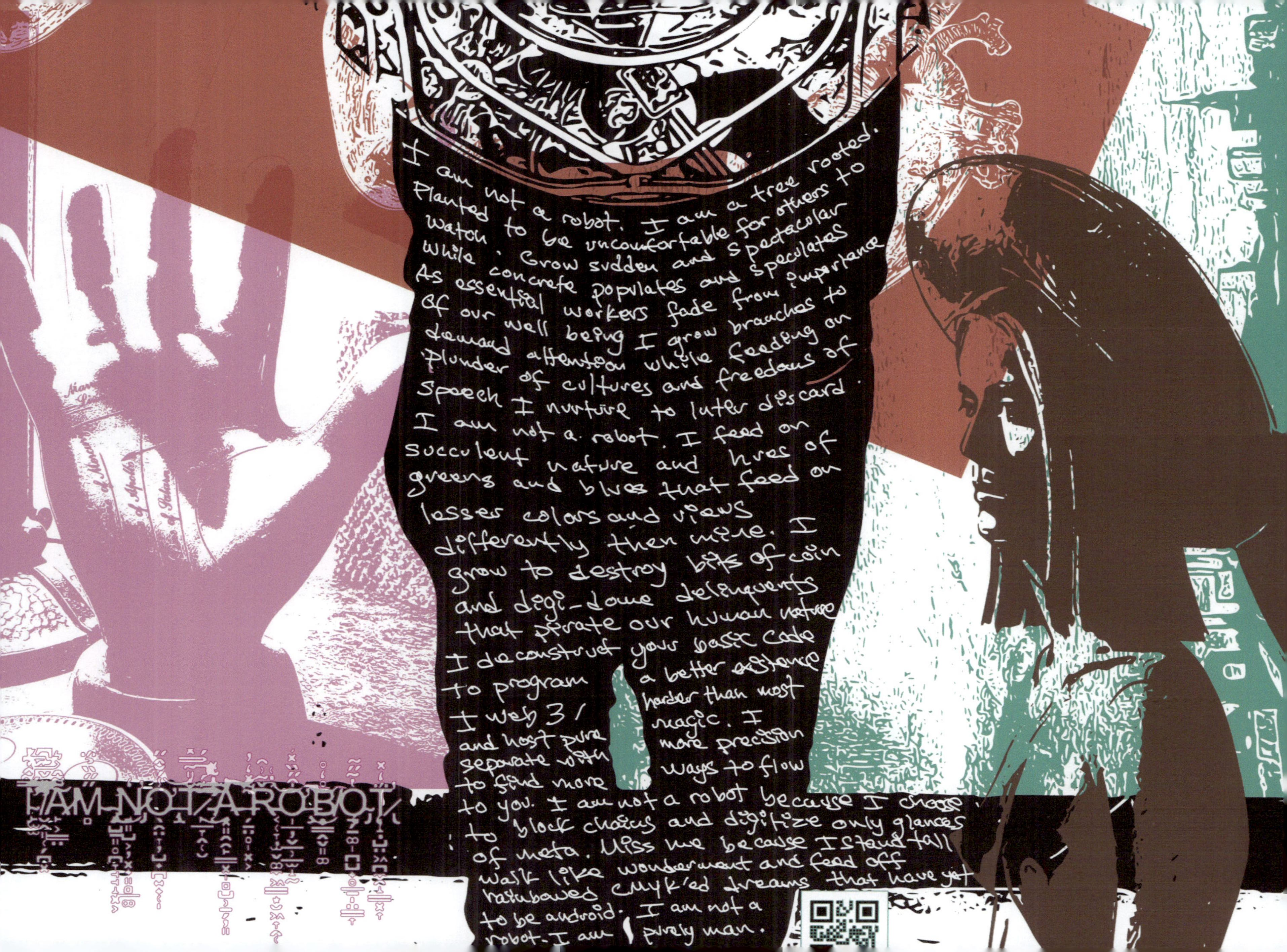

I am not a robot. I am a tree rooted. Planted to be uncomfortable for others to watch. Grow sudden and spectacular while concrete populates and speculates. As essential workers fade from importance of our well being I grow branches to demand attention while feeding on plunder of cultures and freedoms of speech I nurture to later discard. I am not a robot. I feed on succulent nature and hues of greens and blues that feed on lesser colors and views differently then mine. I grow to destroy bits of coin and degi-dome delinquents that pirate our human nature I deconstruct your basic code to program a better existence harder than most magic. I web 3/ and host pure separate with to find more more precision ways to flow to you. I am not a robot because I choose to block choices and digitize only glances of meta. Miss me because I stand tall walk like wonderment and feed off rainbowed cmyk'ed dreams that have yet to be android. I am not a robot. I am purely man.
I AM NOT A ROBOT

ROBOT

I am not a robot.
I am a tree rooted
Planted to be uncomfortable
For others to watch
Grow sudden and spectacular
While concrete populates and speculates
As essential workers
Fade from importance
Of our well being
I grow branches to demand attention
While feeding on plunder of cultures
And freedoms of speech
I nurture to later discard.
I am not a robot
I feed on succulent nature
And hues of greens and blues that
Feed on lesser colors and views
Differently than mine.
I grow to destroy bits of coin
And digi-dome delinquents
That pirate our human nature
I deconstruct your basic code
To program a better existence
I web 3 times harder than most
And host pure magic
I separate with more precision to find
More ways to flow to you
I am not a robot
Because I choose to block chains
And digitize only glances of meta
Miss me because I stand tall
Walk like wonderment and feed off
rainbowed CMYK'ed dreams
That have yet to be android
I am not a robot
I am purely man
I am purely me.

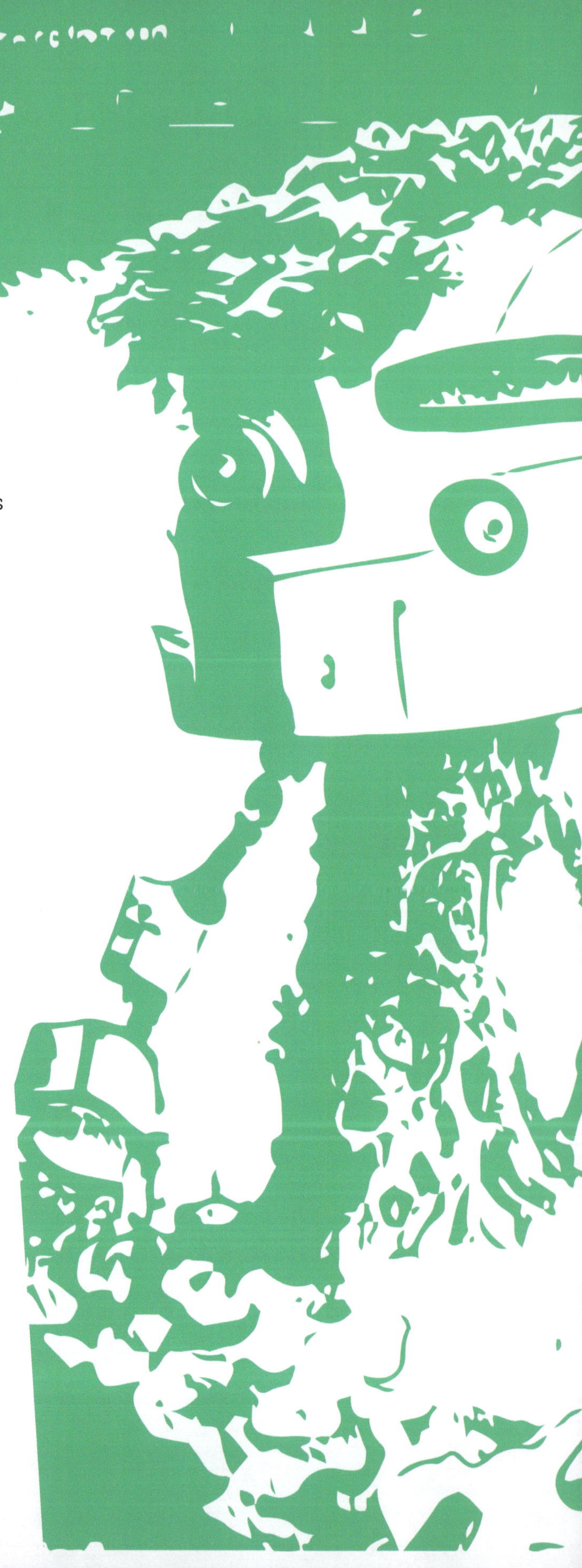

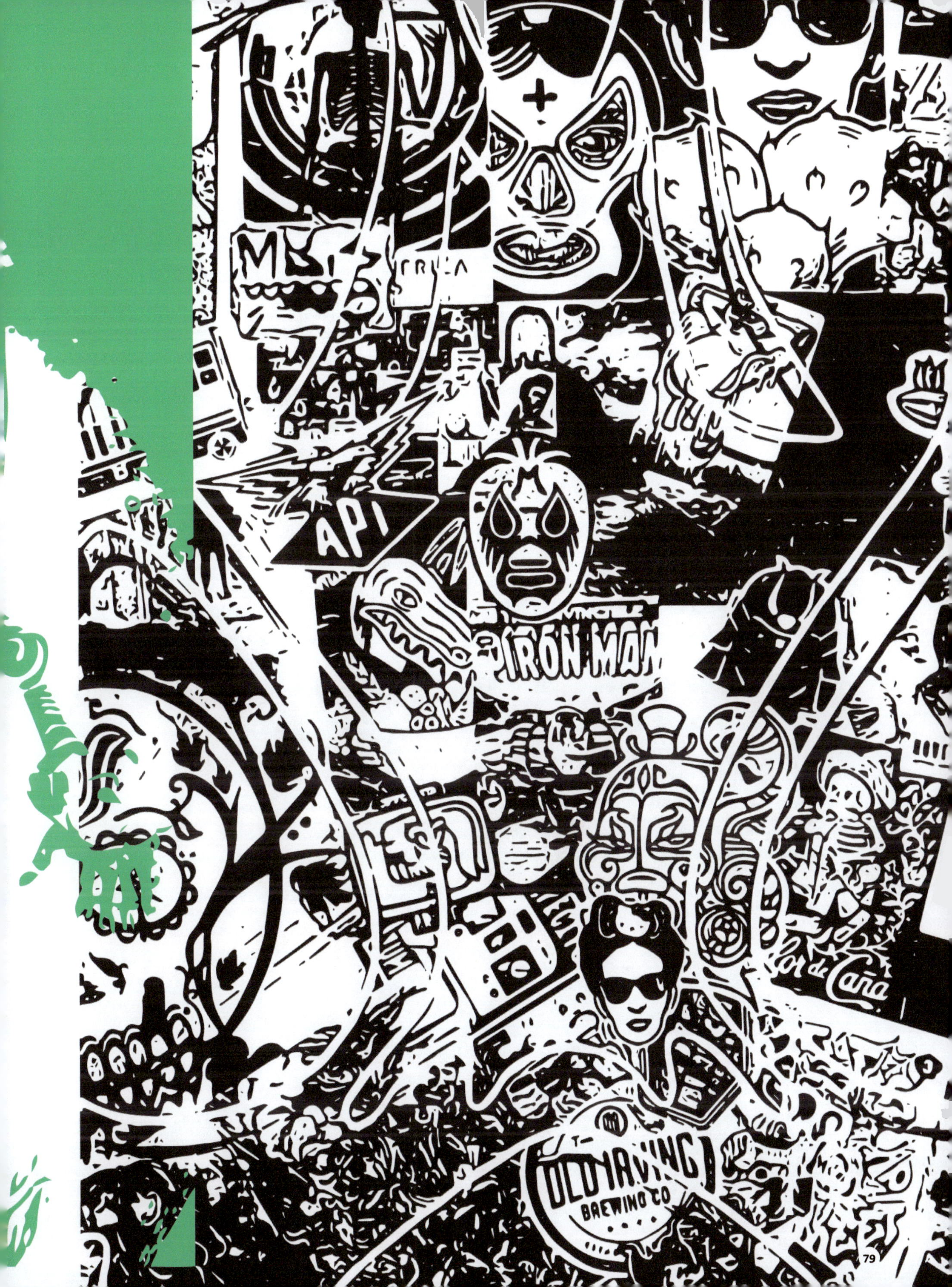

API
IRON MAN
OLD YARVING
BREWING CO

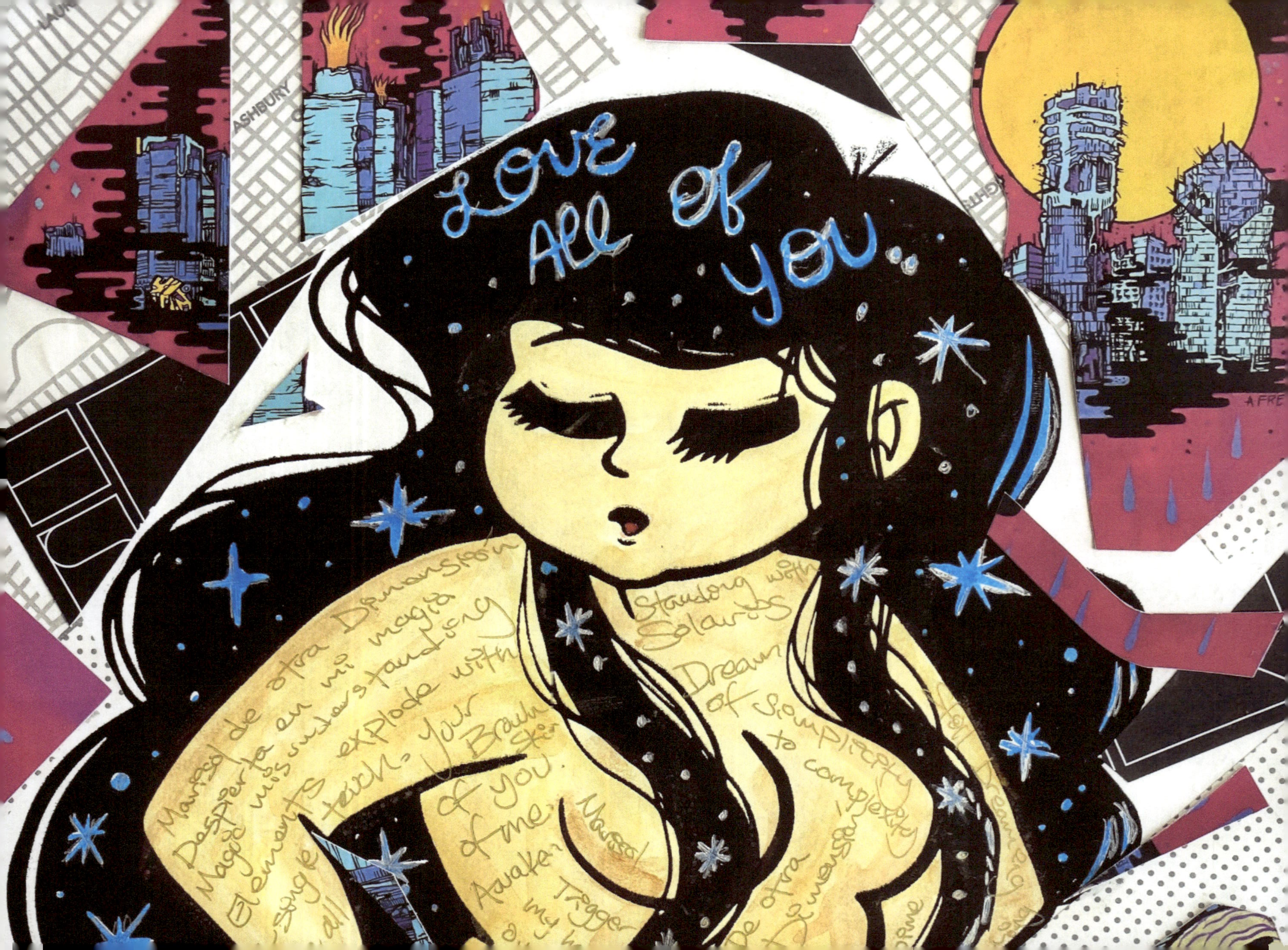

LOVE ALL OF YOU
Marisol de otra Dimension
Despierta en mi magia
Magia misunderstanding
Elements explode with
song teach, your
Brain skin
of you
of me,
Awaken
Trigger my
Standing with
Solaries
Dream of Simplicity to complexity

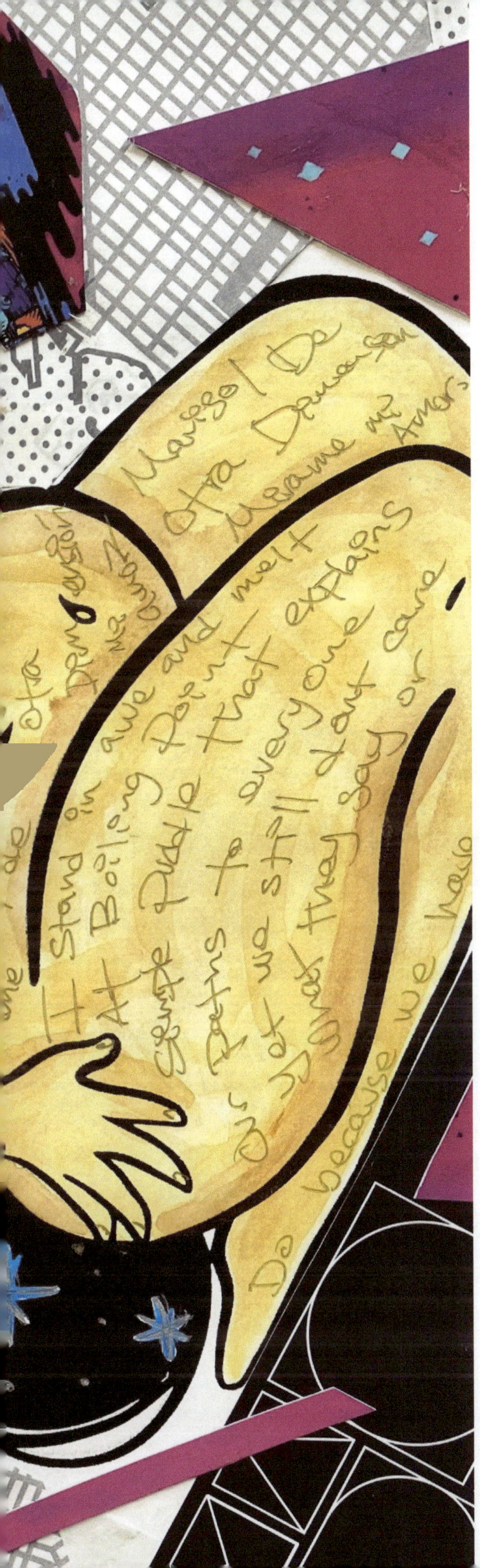

MARISOL

Marisol de otra dimensión
Despierta en mi magia
Magic misunderstanding
Mission biased
Standing with Solaris
Elements explode with
Single touch
Of your brown skin
Favorita
Love all of you
Love all of me
Dream of simplicity
Awaken to complexity
Marisol de otra dimensión
Trigger my happy
Over and over
without trying
Again and again
Free to flow
Without judgement
Marisol de otra dimensión
Mírame
I stand in awe
and melt at boiling point
Simple puddle
Puzzled
That explains
Our paths to everyone
Yet we still don't care
What the *otros*
Say or do
Because we have each other
Marisol de otra dimensión
Mírame mi amor.

TIP JAR TACOS

Chicago summer *viento*
Was keeping me cold like *refresco*
Swimming in plastic bags
Trapped and without shape
I decided to ditch my mind
body and *bolsa*
It was just weighing me down
So I joined the *fiesta*
Familiar beats with teeth
Howled, hungered and *solo*
Led me to you
You slapped me
Called me a *perro*
Then apologized
I took it well
Only because I didn't
remember your name
But your skin was familiar
Like *leche* and Chips Ahoy
Your hand left an imprint
On my out of body self
And it stung
Salsa bien picosa
On tip jar tacos and sangria
Bien fría y roja
Como corazón tirado
Yes, my heart laid on the grass
I haven't picked it up yet
Don't look at me like that
It being there helps
Sooth sweet samples
Rhymes and break beats
Teach me
Certain things at 3am
Taquerías should all be open at that time.
When I blink
I'm trying to forget and remember.
Sangria is best served cold
and shared with friends. .

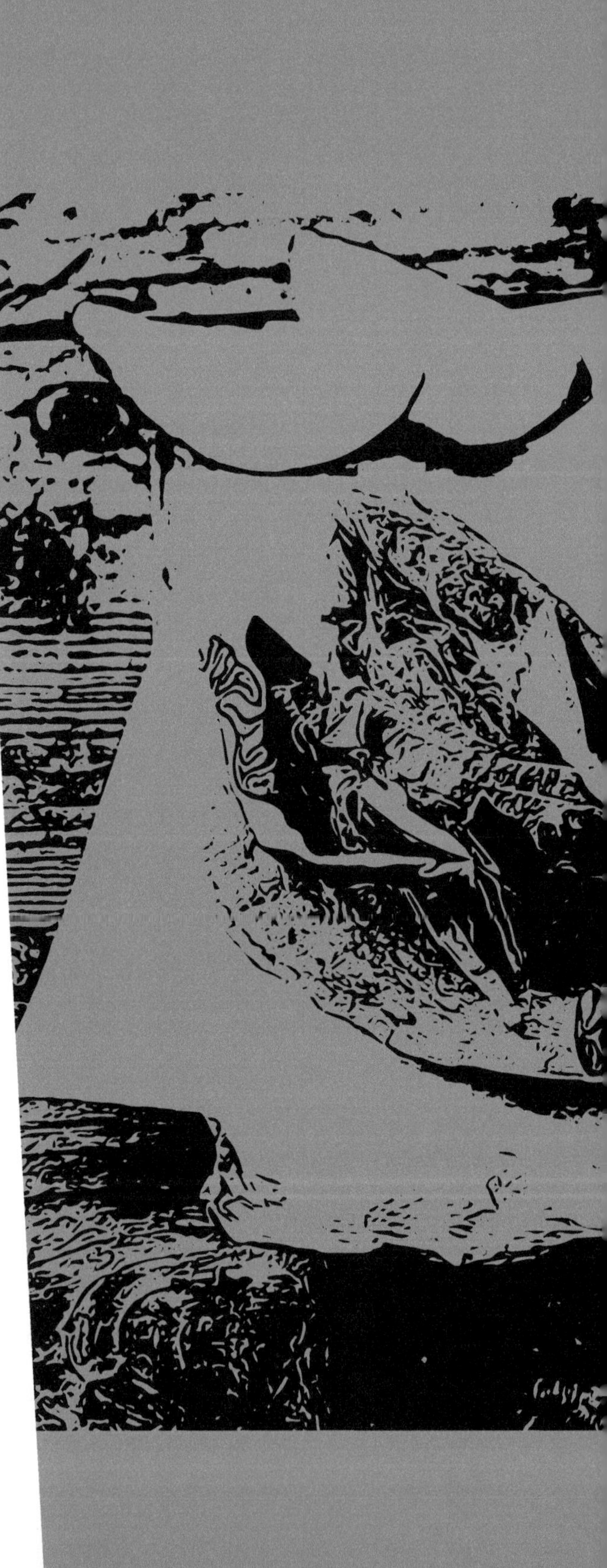

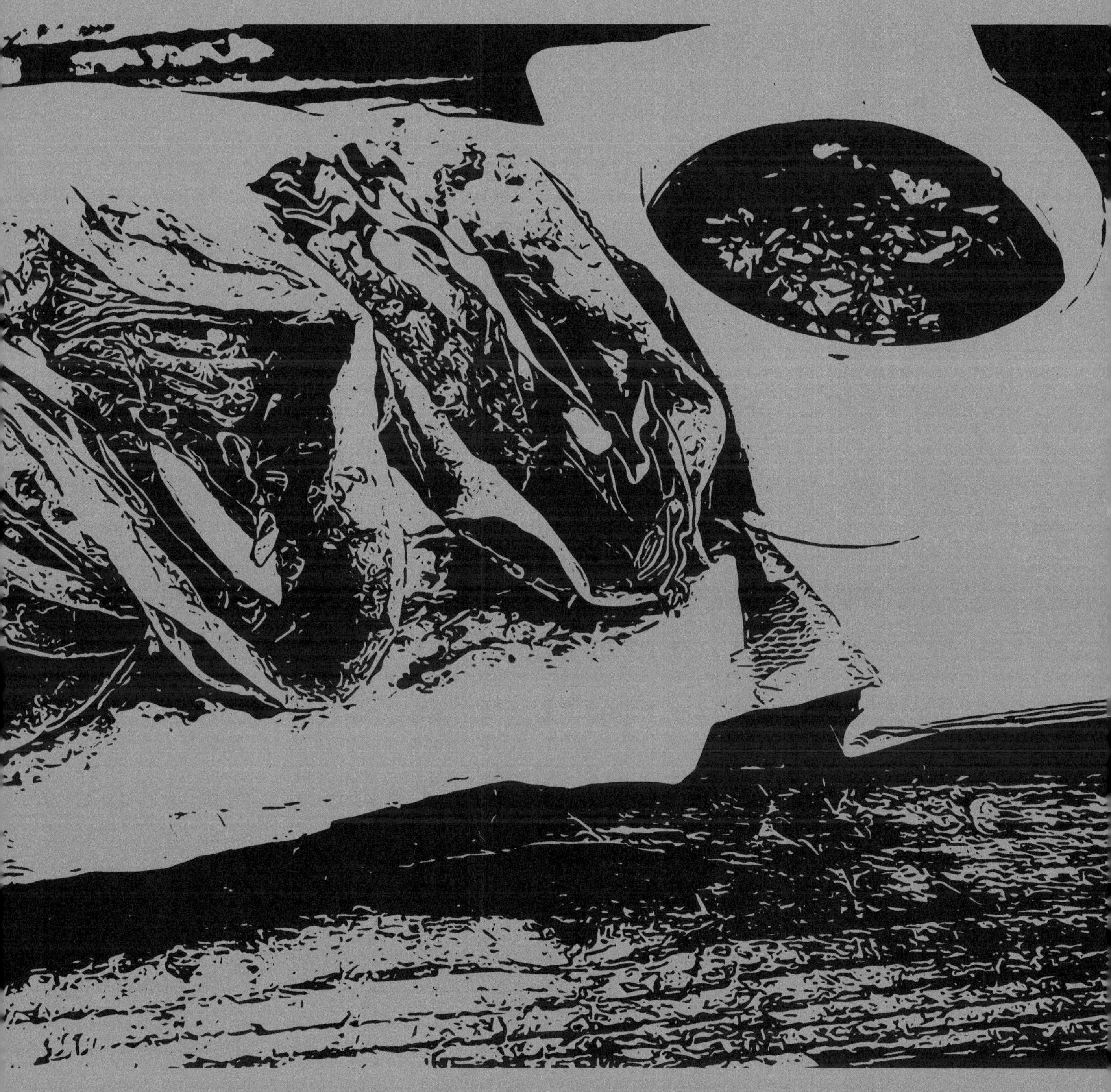

CULTURAL RAPE

Proud, proudly I sat there
Engulfed in rage
Prepared to battle
Anger dictating the movements
my fingers made
Balled up
Stiffening knuckles made up my fist
Veins never seen before
Pulsating against tightening muscle
My face slightly tilted at an angle
I was proud.
Proud like the eagle
That floats and dances
On the flag I like to call my own
But like the eagle
I know no boundaries
No countries
Except one
And from that one we can't escape
Like my mother once did
Laboring against the
"greatest country in the world"
Yet never did she forget
What she left behind
Overwhelming endless beauty
She carries with her
Always bragging
Saying she wants to return
To what? I ask myself
Before I can answer I realize
My true enemy
The poison
I'm about to battle with
My mind
Questions revolving to and fro
Visions
Orchestrations of planned murder
Government fighting,
killing their own culture
Forgetting they came from the same
Indian blood

Boiling over
Forcing them to take up arms
Again
Against corrupt politicians
A country in a state of hectic shock
An altered, revolutionary state
The Indians crying, screaming
It's cultural rape.
They are not alone
The mighty Aztec warrior
heart, soul, dreams
Weeps and whimpers on his knees
Arms raised
Praying to the gods
Saluting for survival
Poisoned arrows waiting patiently
Arrows that can pierce the sky
And part clouds
Till it greets the sun
And makes it bleed cosmic red reasoning
As it floats gently into nothingness
Yet it still has time to warn the moon
To watch out for this warrior
The warrior
thinks not to harm the moon
It needs its light to see
See the light reflect against the pale faces
of white America
Brainwashing with capitalistic expression
a sweet revenge
The *Mexica* soldier tasting it
Licking his fingers
As he pulls back the bow
Staring through the blue
yonder of their eyes
The string flings forward
The arrow flies
A sweet killing
Not a mistake or creation of hate
It's only self defense
From cultural rape.

original image by Sal Vega

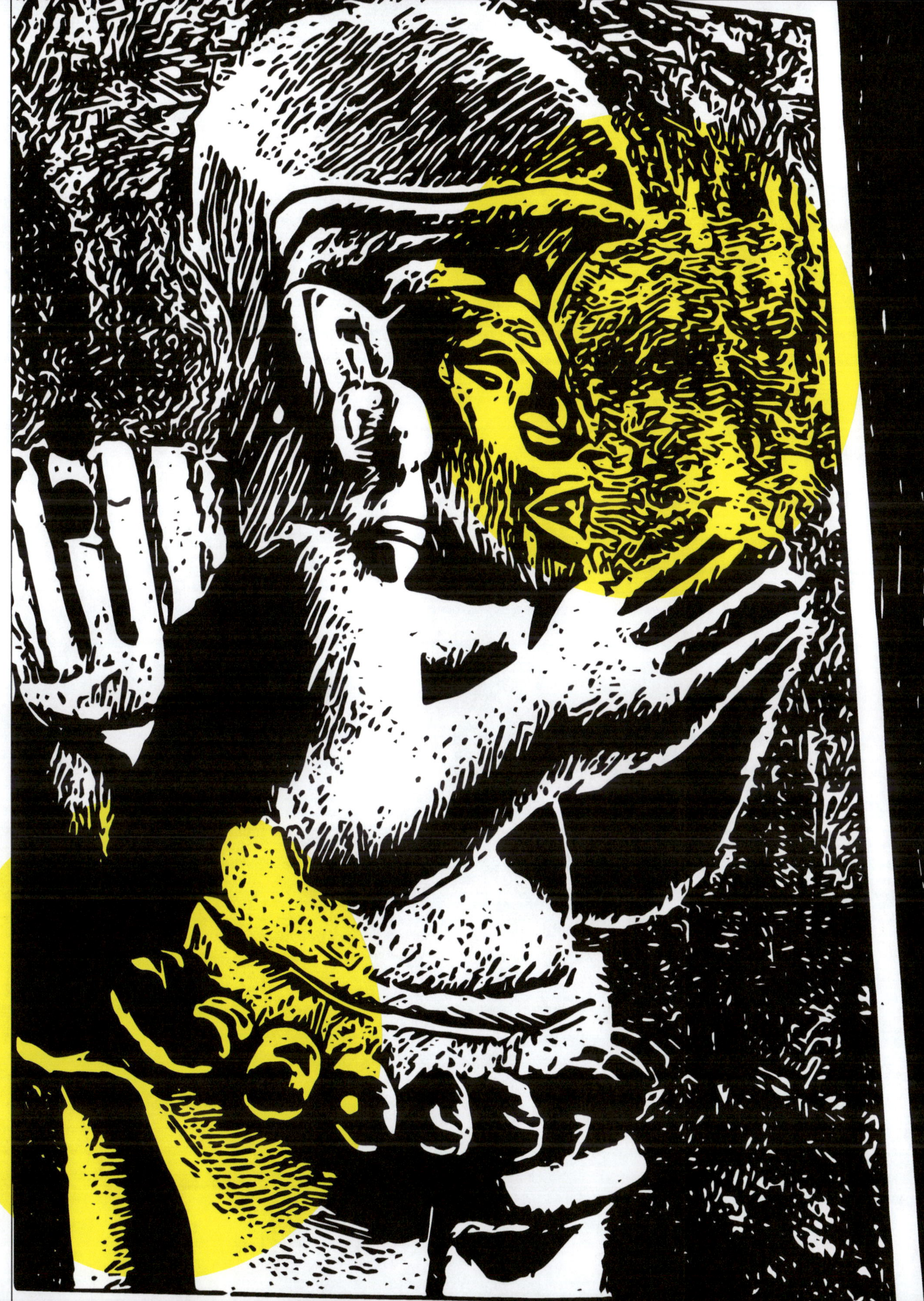

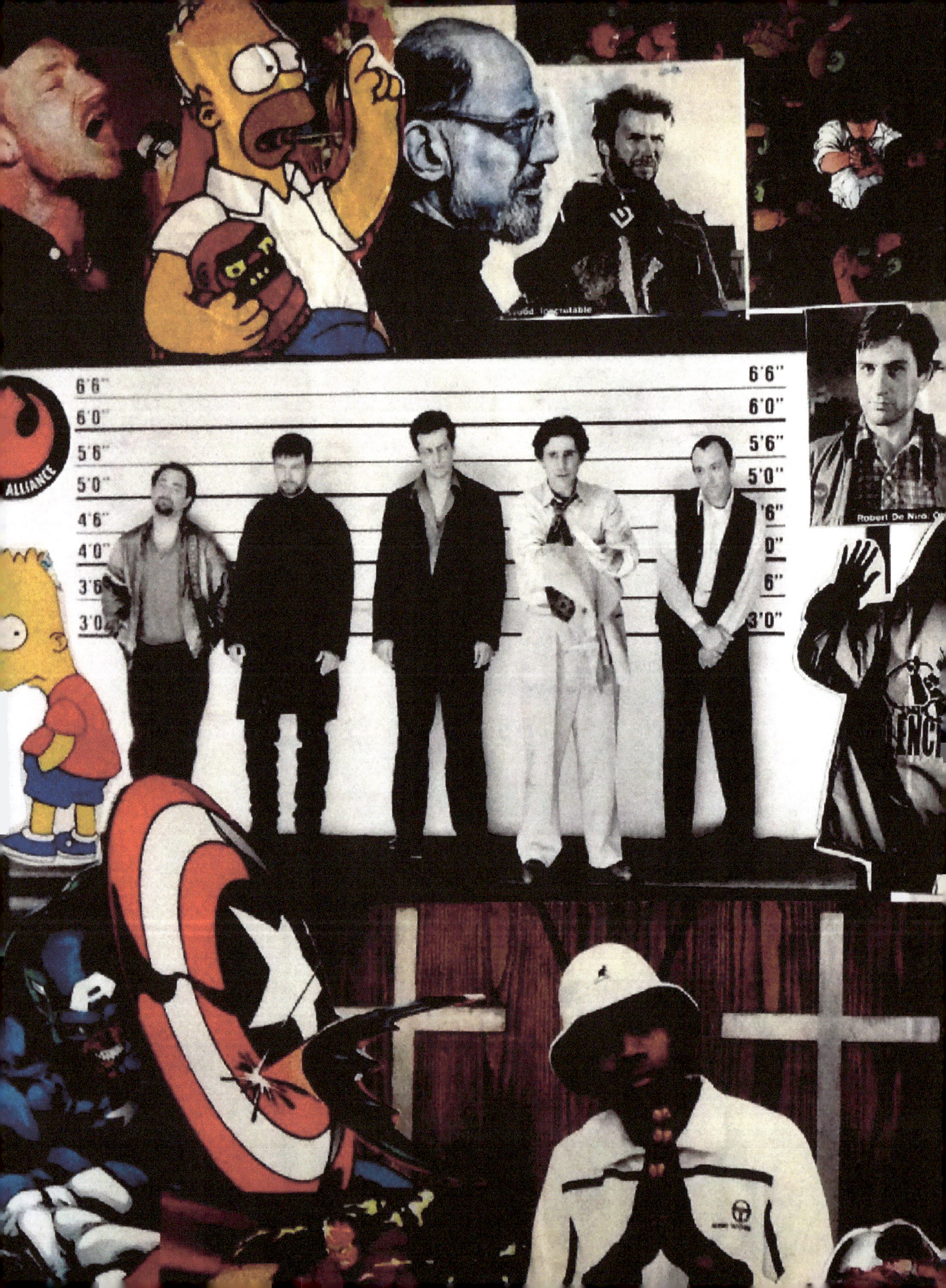

Inscrutable
Robert De Niro
6'6"
6'0"
5'6"
5'0"
4'6"
4'0"
3'6"
3'0"
ALLIANCE

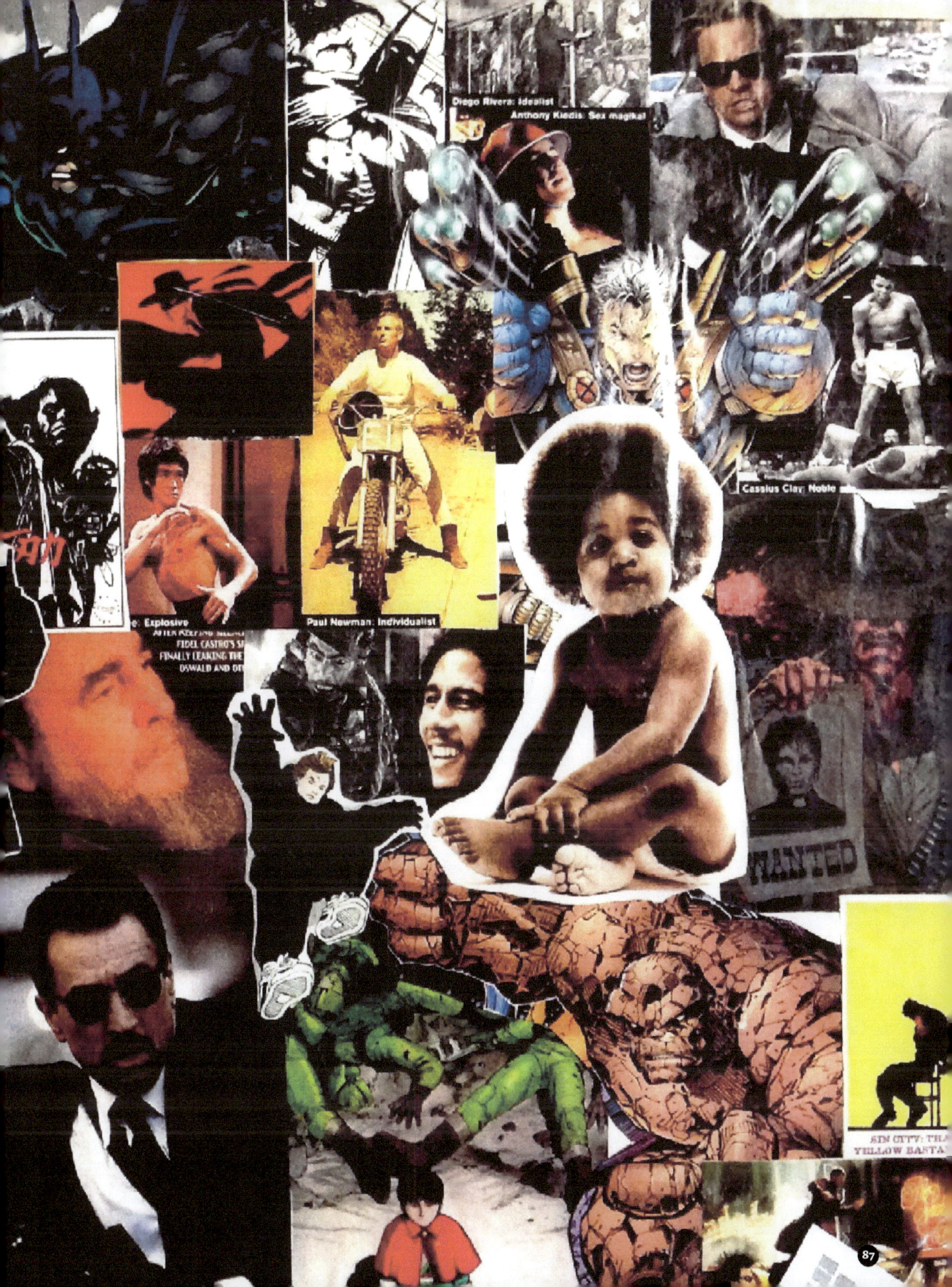

Diego Rivera: Idealist
Anthony Kiedis: Sex magikal
Cassius Clay: Noble
...e: Explosive
AFTER RELEASING RECORDS
FIDEL CASTRO'S S...
FINALLY LEAKING THE...
OSWALD AND OT...
Paul Newman: Individualist
WANTED
SIN CITY: THE
YELLOW BASTA...

LAST WEEK

Text, text ,text
Tonight... How about morning, 4:30
Text, text, text
Tinley, text, text
See you soon
Promise kept
You flip flopped my A.M.
And woke up my art
I drove you to the brink
We benched hummingbirds and cardinals
They played, we followed suit
You drain me and fill me up
You drain me and fill me up
You drain me and fill me up
So we share 159th St.
That's about as far south
as I like sharing by the way
And Waveland was fun.
You made me drink Old Styles
And shared our luck for three hours.
I cup-caked you
And you scared that zombie
when you ran from him
You drain me and fill me up
You drain me and fill me up
You drain me and fill me up
Bible interlude
Pablo 23
You inhabit my eyes
I lack everything
You make me lie
Down with pink pastures
You lead me by frenzied black oceans
You refresh my soul
You drain me and fill me up
You drain me and fill me up
You drain me and fill me up
But damn you are hot, scorching
Como Arizona
Mexicans go to die there or get arrested
Or get arrested

Detained, deported
Or both, wanted or unwanted
My eyes stayed focused
You drain me and fill me up
You drain me and fill me up
You drain me and fill me up
Divorce your body
Marry my mind, Sever my hands
So I can't hold your fingertips
Touch is sculpted
Feelings scripted
You bite your bottom lip
I blink and bite that same spot
And linger and I believe you
And can't stop
You drain me and fill me up
You drain me and fill me up
You drain me and fill me up
You warn me
I disregard
My Casio breaks
We disregard
I retire and un-retire
You just quit
But only temporarily
But at least you apply
And that means something
So I look for a piggy bank
But can't find one big enough
So you strand me
Drain me
Text, talk
Cop let us go
Talk, Text, text
Walk,walk
Talk
Hate, hate
Text, text, text
No reply.
At least you drove me back. .

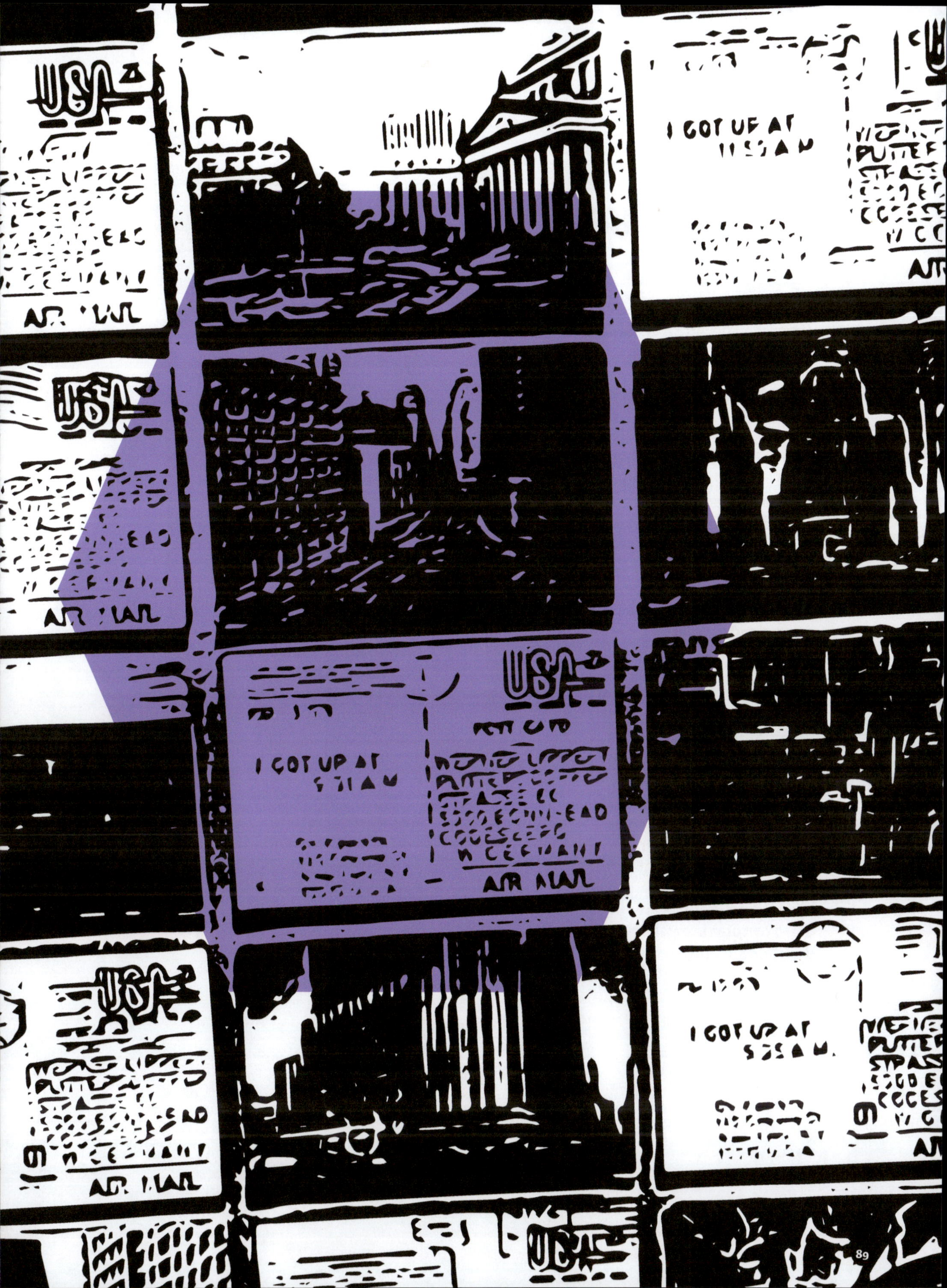

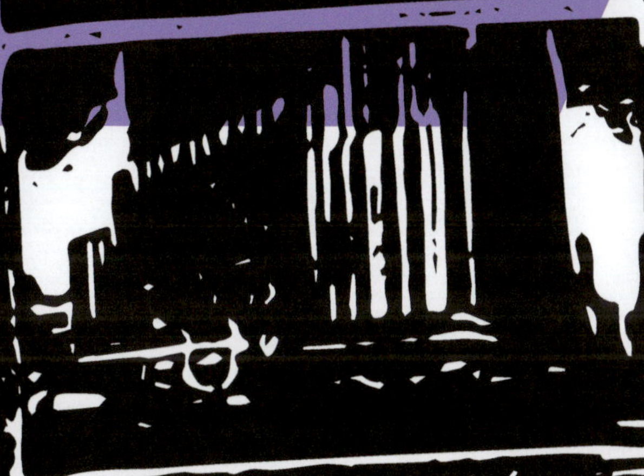
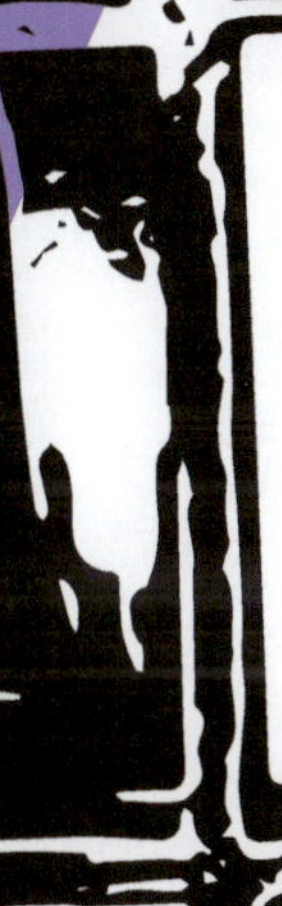
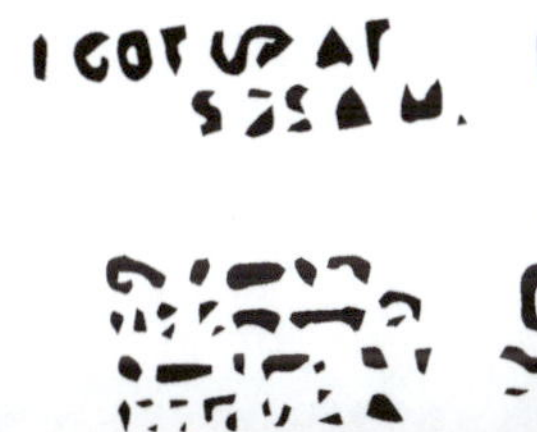
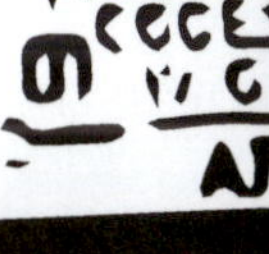
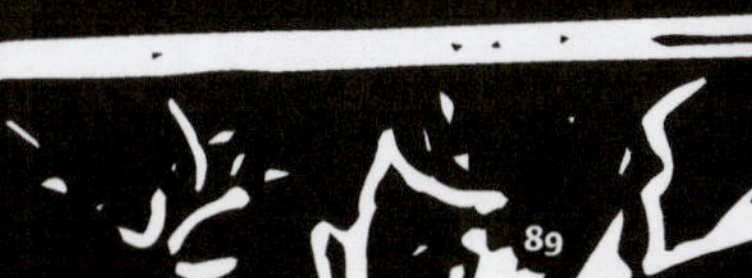

QUETZALCÓATL

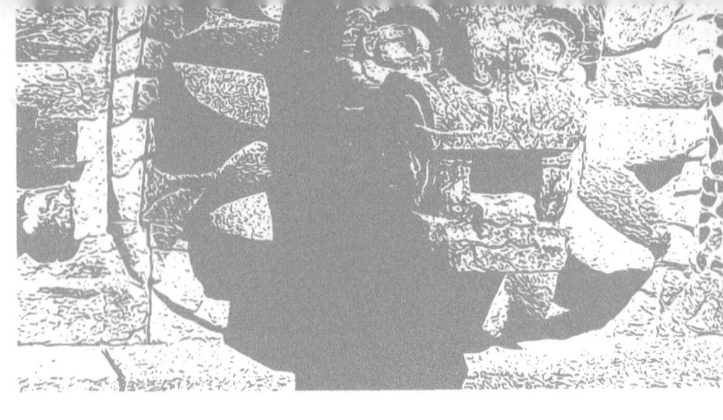

I walk on the rooftops
Because the sidewalk sizzles
But wouldn't it be nice to fly
Explore
Even just for a day
un día solo
Porque las calles apestan
A tristeza, Miller y desmadre
Colas arrastrando pero en rumbo
A trabajar las 80 horas
Para completar pa la renta
Y los bill-es y la taquiza
Del cumple del primo Carlos
Pero quiero bailar
Quetzalcóatl
Dios de los dioses
De los vientos
De vida
De Venus
Y de la mañana
Regálame alas
For a day
So i can whisper to my ancestors
So I can dance on rooftops
De mis barrios
And get a little browner
So my *gente* never questions
Mi nopal
Regálame viento
Para limpiar las calles de los
Políticos y burgueses

Y los vasos vacíos
Give me strong lungs
So that I can forgive
Words that are meant to harm
Disarm and protect
Diablitos que andan
Haciendo travesuras
Regálame tu maíz
Para sembrar
Libros y poesía
Arte y cultura
Pinturas y escultura
Tortillas y frijoles
Borrachos
En las esquinas
That loved just like us
But now are forgotten
Regálame tu collar
Para escuchar la armonía
De las conchas marinas
Carefully woven to protect
Talisman
And maybe I can use them
To blind with beauty
And *turquesa*
Transform through peace
As I dance on rooftops
And sing about *abuelitas*

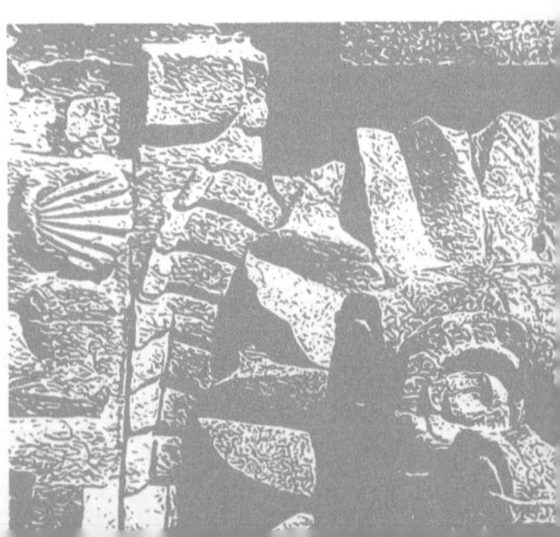

Regálame tus plumas
Para borrar los mal
entendimientos
Entre familias
Sobre dioses y diferencias
Feather my landing because
These blues, greens and purples
Have me drowning in city lights
Contaminated by metal shredders
And social media *pendejadas*
Quetzalcóatl
Regálame tus dientes
Para saborear mi futuro
Y morder mis maldades
Fear my fangs
So that I am never mistaken
For being weak
Or for wearing
My heart on sleeve
Today I dance on rooftops
Porque me dejas
Before you disappear
Mi Quetzalcóatl.

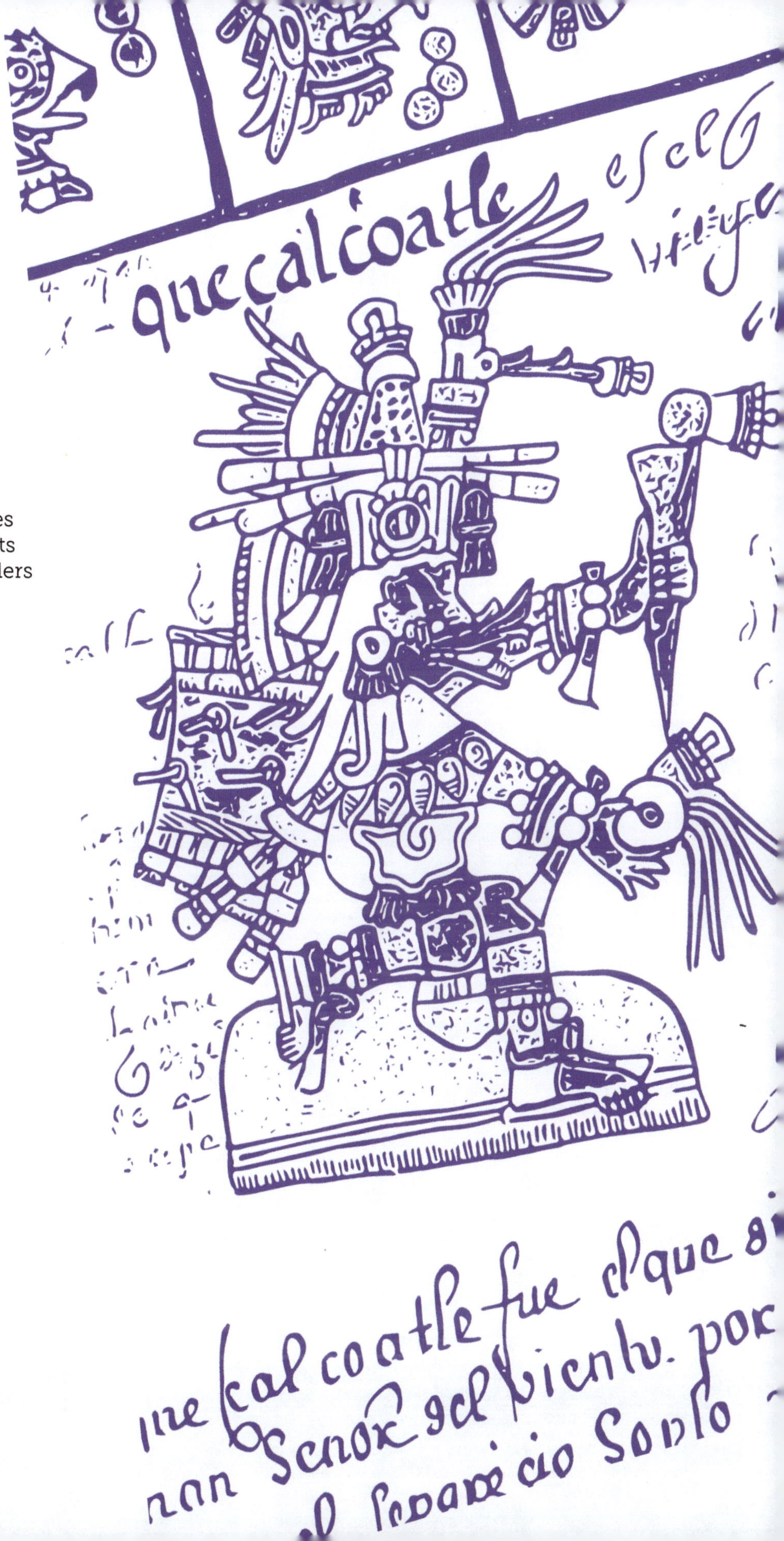

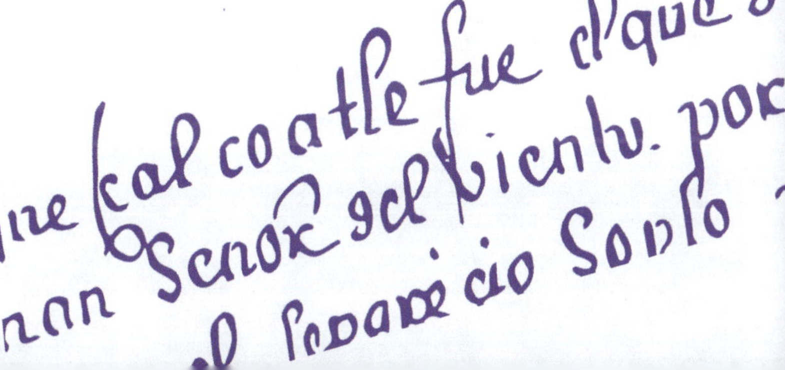

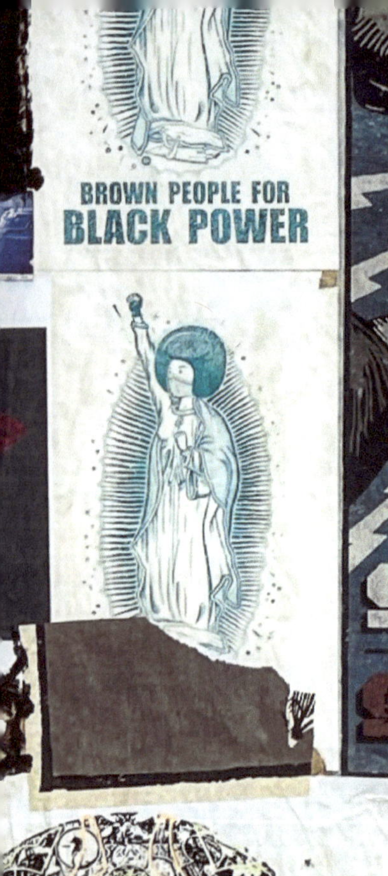

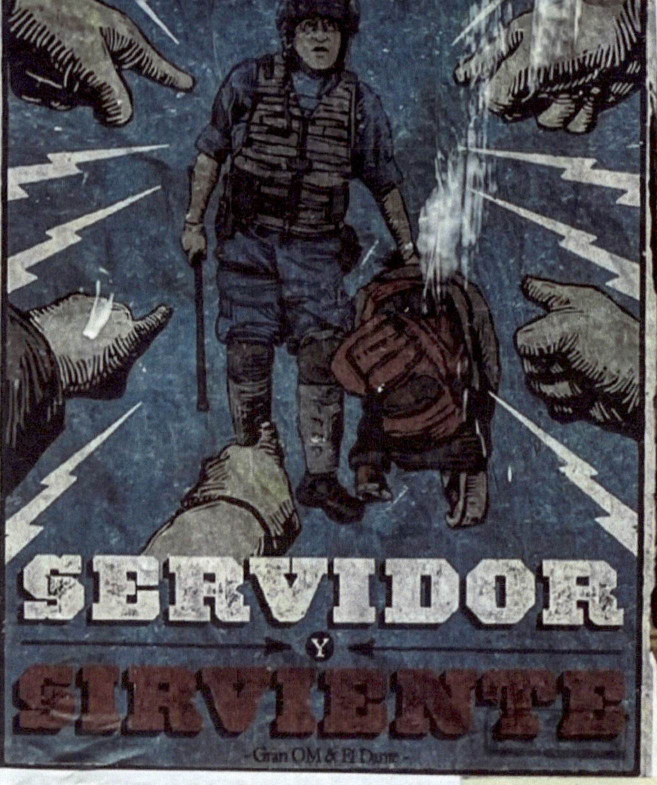

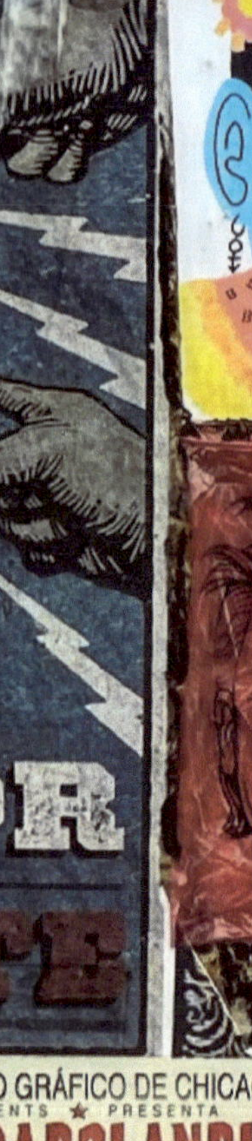

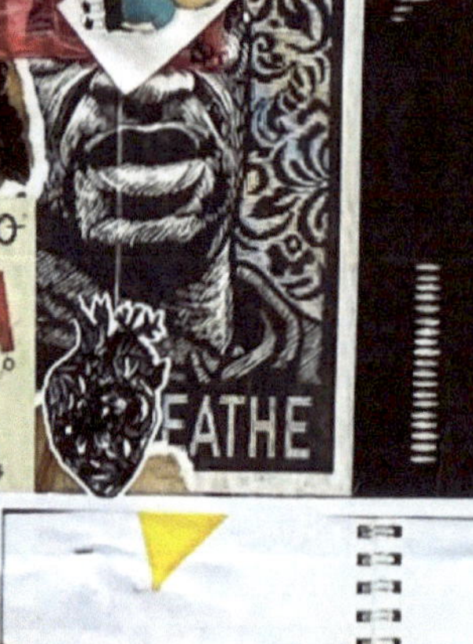

DR. MILAGROS

Pilsen pray for me
Teach me your wicked ways
Disassemble my insides
Abolish my gentry
Love my passion
Steal my color
Dream for me
Save me from myself
Set politics aside but vote
Believe in yourself
Dime que me quieres
Respetame! Destroy me
Delicious pero cuentame despues
Cuanto me quieres
Spit on me but open the door
Love my brownness
Heart my Blackness
Destroy my gamut
Lets see each others spectrum
Because you are ugly
But I love you
Mi querido Pilsen.

@1000MASKS

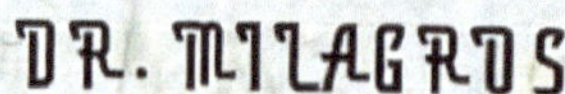

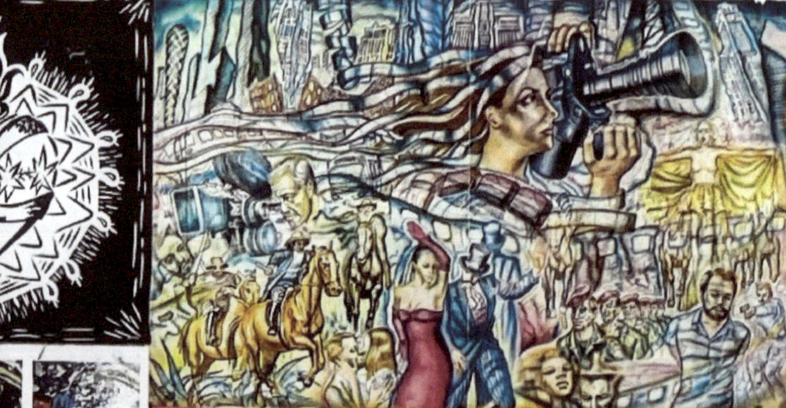

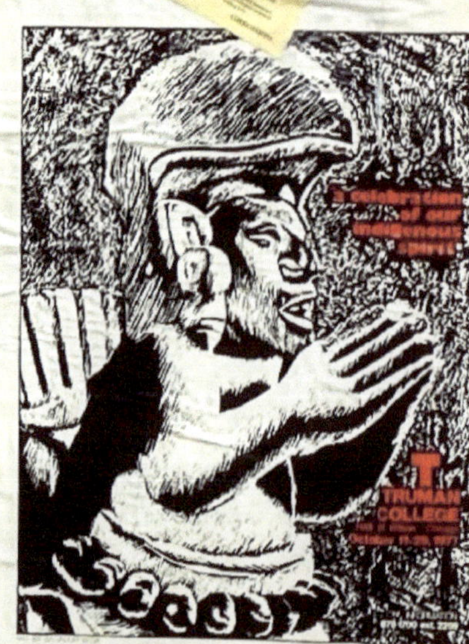

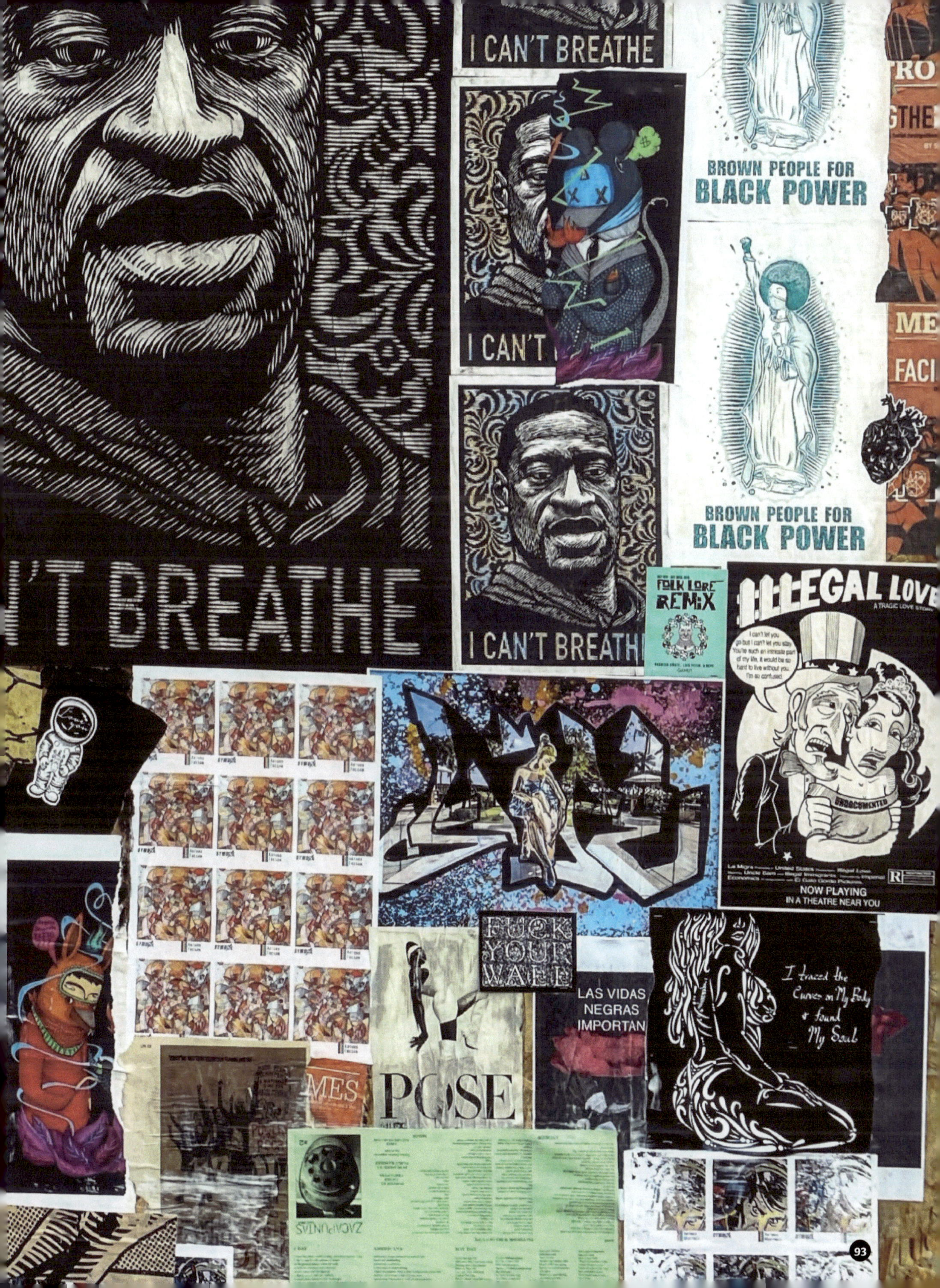

I CAN'T BREATHE
I CAN'T
I CAN'T BREATHE
N'T BREATHE
I CAN'T BREATHE
BROWN PEOPLE FOR
BLACK POWER
BROWN PEOPLE FOR
BLACK POWER
FOLK LORE REMIX
ILLEGAL LOVE
A TRAGIC LOVE STORY
UNDOCUMENTED
NOW PLAYING
IN A THEATRE NEAR YOU
FUCK YOUR WALL
LAS VIDAS NEGRAS IMPORTAN
POSE
I traced the Curves on My Body & found My Soul
TRO
THE
ME
FACI
ZACAPUNTAS

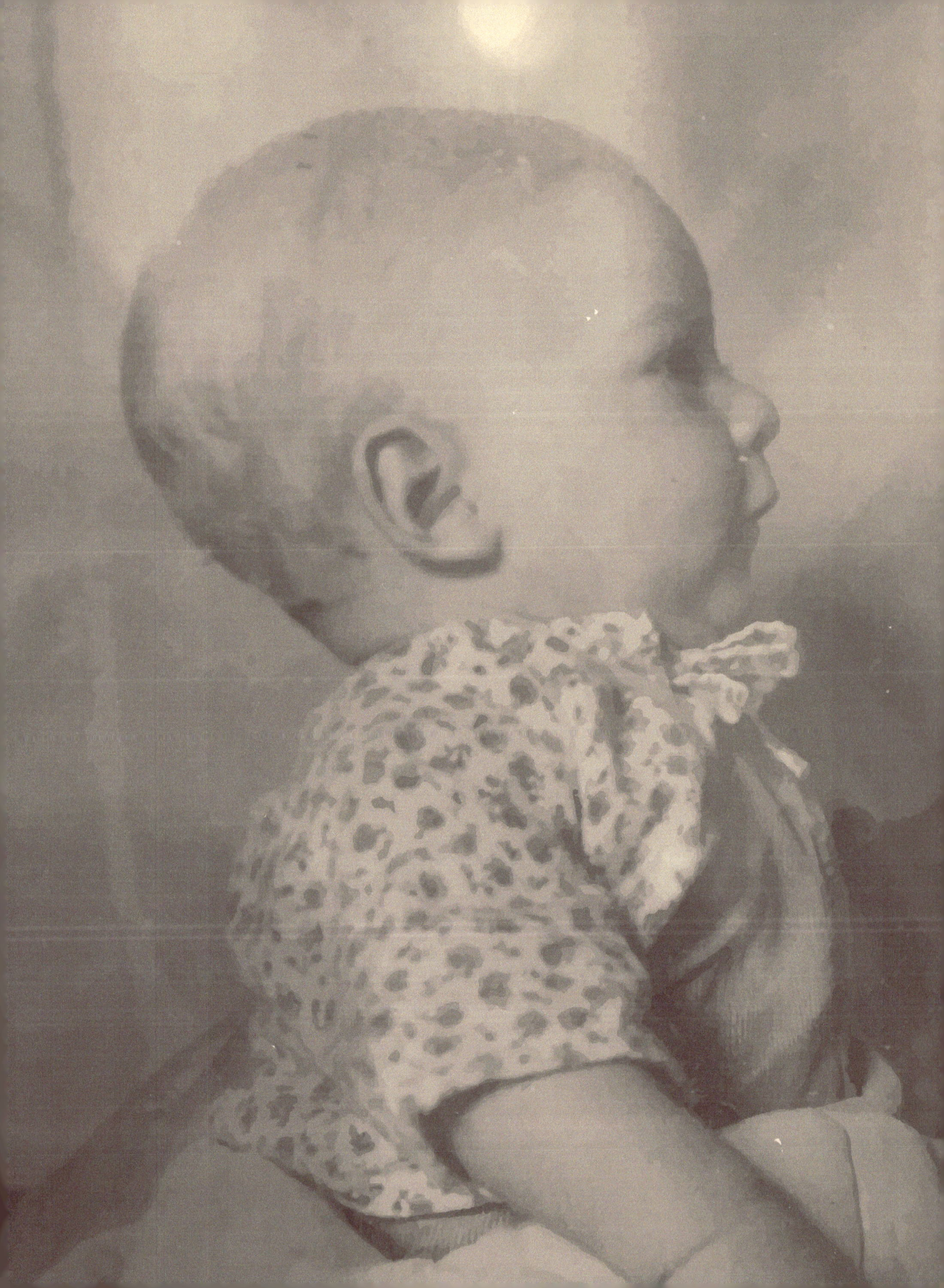

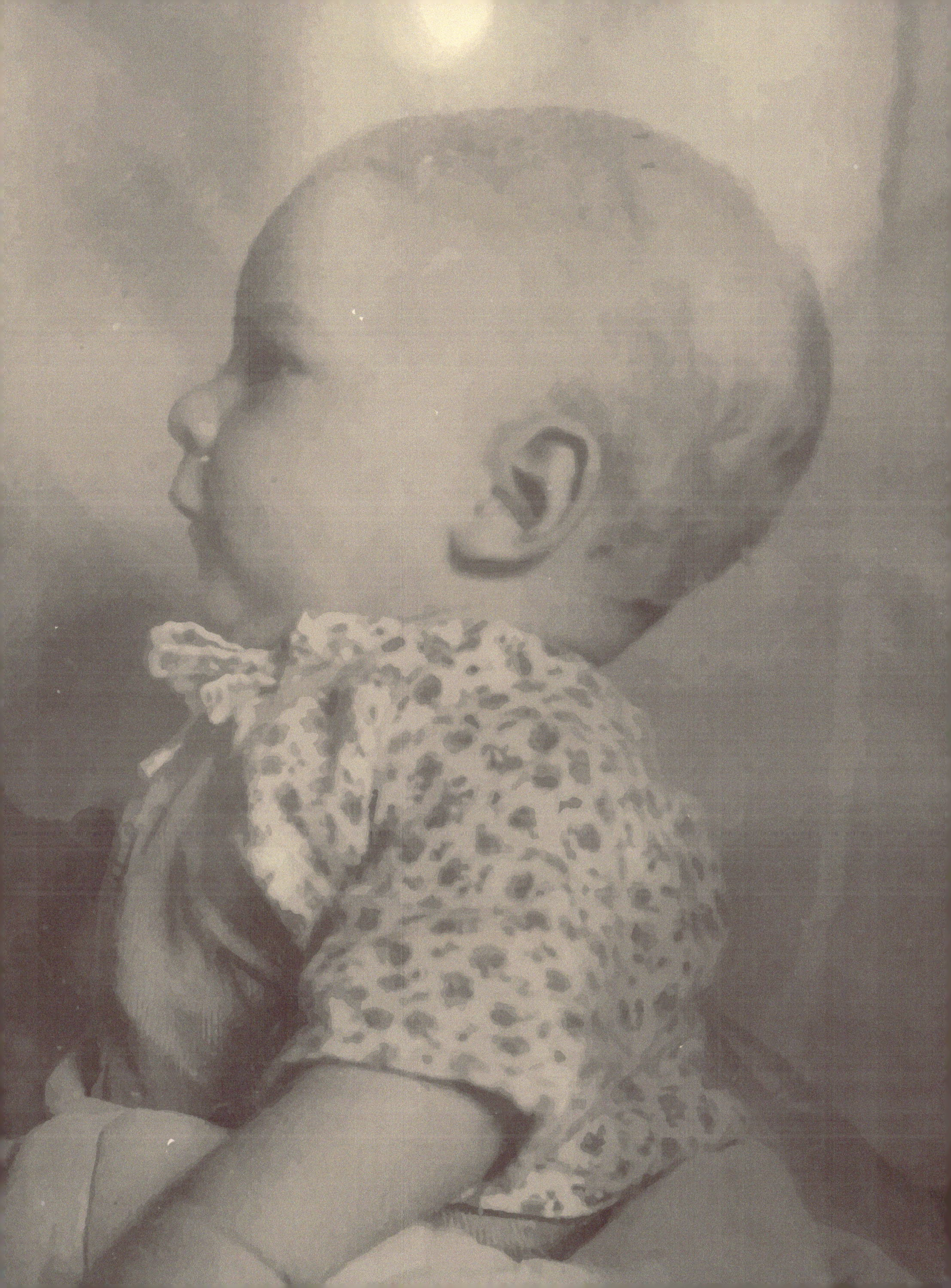

THANKS & ACKNOWLEDGEMENTS

To my partner Teresa
My primos
My parientes
Mi familia especialmente Martita

To the poets that inspired me
The painters that gave me colors to play with
To the muralists that taught me respect
To the graff artists that taught me about locations
And handstyles
To street artists that made me
laugh and question
Am I doing enough
To my printmakers that
taught me courage
and how to use black
To my breakers and dj's and mc's
That gave me my youth and my escape
To all teachers that wake up to make dreamers
To my homies that flood the streets with stickers
To all the pirates that share
knowledge and understanding
To anyone that's opened a
gallery/cultural space in the hood
To help give voices and opportunities to creatives
To my organizer family that builds through union
And collective strength in numbers
To my ancestors that fought
for everything we have.
Nuestra Cultura!

Gracias.

Would like to thank all the artists,musicians,photographers, whose art has appeared in my original collages. Artwork is sourced from postcards, comics, stickers, magazines, posters that I have collected over the last 30 years of my life. Posters are all designed by me to share with my city that I love and are often found on streets as part of public art and public discourse. Special thanks to Wu-Tang Clan, MF DOOM RIP, Biggie RIP, Tribe, De-La,Gang Starr,RATM, Soundgarden,RHCP, Dinosaur Jr., Sade and Radiohead for all the vibes. Gratitude for all the people that looked over the many versions of the book like Marta Ayala, Citlali López Ortiz, Javier Suarez, Marc Zimmerman, Diana Solís,Carlos Cumpián and Luis Urrea.